America as Overlord

AMERICA
AS OVERLORD
From World War Two to the Vietnam War

HAL DRAPER
Foreword by Samuel Farber

Haymarket Books
Chicago, Illinois

© 2011 Center for Socialist History
Foreword © 2023, Samuel Farber

Originally published in 2011 by Center for Socialist History in Alameda, California.

This edition published in 2023 by
Haymarket Books
P.O. Box 180165
Chicago, IL 60618
773-583-7884
www.haymarketbooks.org
info@haymarketbooks.org

ISBN: 978-1-64259-848-3

Distributed to the trade in the US through Consortium Book Sales and Distribution (www.cbsd.com) and internationally through Ingram Publisher Services International (www.ingramcontent.com).

This book was published with the generous support of Lannan Foundation and Wallace Action Fund.

Special discounts are available for bulk purchases by organizations and institutions. Please email info@haymarketbooks.org for more information.

Cover photograph of two F-100D Super Sabre aircraft over South Vietnam, courtesy of American Photo Archive/Alamy Stock Photo.

Cover design by Jamie Kerry.

Library of Congress Cataloging-in-Publication data is available.

10 9 8 7 6 5 4 3 2 1

Contents

Publisher's Note

This collection contains essays written for a number of radical periodicals over the period 1954 to 1969. The earliest essay was written during the Eisenhower administration, which was the political, economic and cultural acme of what publisher Henry Luce called "the American Century." The latest was written when the impending American defeat in Vietnam was about to bring that century to a premature close. The essays are characterized by a unique political analysis of American imperialism in the post World War II period.

The phrase "world policeman" used to describe the role assumed by the American government since the end of World War II had, especially since the fiasco of Vietnam, become a cliche. Cliches can sometimes be useful but this one had not only become hackneyed, it was not quite true.

For one thing, the U.S. was not the policeman in Eastern Europe or Tibet. Others patroled those beats. For another, one of the most important roles of American imperialism in the period covered by these essays was that of arbiter of the internal disputes of the capitalist bloc. The U.S. cannot simply dictate terms to its allies through military and economic might as it, and they, try to do to countries in what has come to be called the Third World.

Capitalism has required such an arbiter since at least the Second World War because a social revolution followed that war in the former colonial possesions of the European powers. In the first decade or so after the war capitalism was threatened even in Europe and Japan. Fratricidal, civilization-threatening disasters like the first and second world wars were clearly too dangerous. By default, the U.S. became the overlord and arbiter required. It alone had sufficient economic and military muscle.

The existence of a rival anticapitalist social system in the form of bureaucratic collectivism which was also capable of intervening in world politics strengthened the U.S. position even more. None of this precluded the U.S. and the other capitalist states from pursuing their colonialist and neocolonialist rackets as recklessly as before; it was just *because* of the competition among the capitalist states induced by this recklessness that the services of an overlord were required. To further complicate matters, the U.S. itself throughout this period engaged in some of the more outrageous acts of international lawlessness, thus giving aid and comfort politically to the common enemy of the capitalist bloc. If the U.S. was the regulator of world capitalism then who regulated the U.S. itself?

Nevertheless, the most brutal and characteristic acts of American aggression in this period were in defense of the common interests of the "free world". The protracted, politically and economically exhausting war in Vietnam cannot be explained by any *immediate* U.S. interest. Its ability to defend capitalism and its dependents from social revolution was being called into question. This conception of the U.S. as arbiter and overlord of the capitalist bloc is outlined theoretically in the second essay which, indeed, sets the theme for this collection.

The dates and names of the periodicals are appended to the individual essays. Each essay is introduced by a brief note recalling the context in which it was written. The essays themselves have not been revised or changed, and the reader may well run into references that time has rendered dim. But we believe that the main lines of analysis remain as clear, and as important, as they were when the writing was done.

In the 21st century, with the collapse of any serious rival, the contradiction between the tasks facing the world's "last remaining super power" and the mental and political capacities of its governing class, the contradiction pointed to in the second essay in this anthology, is greater than ever.

Center for Socialist History

Foreword

Samuel Farber

By the time I first met Hal Draper in 1963 when I was a new graduate student in the sociology department at UC Berkeley, Hal had been an acquisitions librarian on campus for some time. He studied for this new profession when he was in his forties after moving from New York where he had been for several years the editor of the weekly *Labor Action*, an organ of the Independent Socialist League (ISL).

The ISL was then the current embodiment of a political tendency that traced its origin to a political break with Leon Trotsky: Trotsky characterized of the USSR as a degenerated workers state that had to be defended against Western imperialism, while at the same time, he argued, a political revolution was necessary to overthrow the Stalinist bureaucracy. The Trotskyist dissidents argued that the USSR had become a new form of class society that they called "bureaucratic collectivism," which had to be overthrown by a revolution that would be not only political but also social, precisely because a new class would have taken power. Moreover, the ISL held that the USSR was not defensible, as Trotsky believed, particularly after it had invaded Finland and allied with Nazi Germany to eliminate Poland as an independent nation in 1939. These foreign invasions in fact originally set in motion the evolving dynamic of the split with Trotsky. Internationally, both the Communist parties that had become entirely subservient to Moscow's interests and the liberal and conservative defenders of capitalism had to be confronted by a revolutionary Third Camp tendency under the slogan "Neither Washington nor Moscow."

I quickly became one of several radical socialist students for whom Hal Draper served as a mentor. For me, Hal became the embodiment of what a Marxist scholar should be. I consulted him on numerous occasions on questions pertaining to the ideas and politics of Karl Marx as well as on the political issues of the day, whether these concerned the labor movement or our position on free speech. One result of this latter consultation was Hal Draper's decision to write a seminal article outlining the grounds for his defense of free speech.[1]

---

1 Hal Draper, "Free Speech and Political Struggle," *Independent Socialist*, no. 4 (April 1968): 12–16, https://www.marxists.org/history/etol/newspape/workerspower/is4.pdf.

As an authentic Marxist, Hal Draper was a political practitioner of the first order, even though I don't recall he ever used the term "praxis," a fashionable term in academic Marxist circles. This became evident in the fall of 1964, exactly a year after I had met him, when the Free Speech Movement broke out on the Berkeley campus. Hal, working closely together with the newly founded Independent Socialist Club (of which he was the main political leader, and I was a member), played a major role in that movement. Besides being a frequent speaker at the FSM rallies, the fifty-year-old Hal Draper played a crucial ideological and political role through his widely disseminated pamphlet *The Mind of Clark Kerr*, an incisive and detailed study of the ideas of the industrial relations professor who had become the president of the University of California. Draper revealed and critically analyzed Kerr's vision of universities becoming a central part of the "knowledge industry," an analysis that was immediately echoed by Mario Savio, the FSM leader, in his famous speech on December 2, 1964, denouncing Kerr's idea of the university as if it were a factory. To combat the university as the factory that Kerr envisaged, Savio exhorted the Berkeley students "to put your bodies upon the gears and upon the wheels . . . upon the levers, upon all the apparatus, and you've got to make it stop."[2]

During that struggle, I also discovered Draper's impressive tactical talents. At the height of the FSM struggle, elections were scheduled for student government, a typical undemocratic "sandbox" institution with close ties to the world of fraternities and sororities from which practically all radical and liberal students stayed away. (Graduate students were excluded from membership for fear of their radicalism.) Draper however, convincingly argued to the skeptical ISC members, myself included, that this time the relation of forces among the students had radically shifted and that the FSM militants and sympathizers should participate in the elections and attempt to take over student government. Indeed, this is what happened, with a decisive vote removing the student government leaders who had opposed the FSM from the beginning.

In the age of postmodernism and assorted non-rational and irrational tendencies, Hal Draper stands as an excellent representative of the left wing of the Enlightenment, in the tradition of Karl Marx, who pursued a rational and revolutionary theory and method of understanding and changing society. Always

---

2 Mario Savio, "Introduction," in *Berkeley. The Student Revolt* by Hal Draper (Chicago: Haymarket Books, 2020), 1–7.

willing to take an unpopular stand when the political situation required it, Draper cut through the soft-headedness common in the American left while at the same time welcoming, encouraging, and praising new radicalizing forces, no matter how politically raw these might have been. Thus, quite in contrast with several of his former ISL comrades such as Irving Howe, the editor of *Dissent,* who were busy castigating and excommunicating the New Leftists, Draper welcomed and defended them in a comradely but critical fashion.[3] Members of the ISC such as myself made copies and widely distributed Draper's article "In Defense of the 'New Radicals'" among fellow young Berkeley radicals.

Without a doubt, Hal Draper's crowning intellectual and political achievement was his multi-volume treatise *Karl Marx's Theory of Revolution* published by Monthly Review Press in the seventies and eighties, after he withdrew from organized active political activity. In a highly erudite but very accessible study of the ideas and actions of Karl Marx, Draper more than convincingly demonstrated that Marx's views on socialist revolution and democracy were inextricably intertwined, thus creating the fundamental basis of what Draper had earlier called "socialism from below."

Political Background to *America as Overlord*

The nine articles in this collection were all published between 1954 and 1969. Although these articles were read by people in many parts of the world, left-wing people in the United States were the primary audience that Hal Draper thought needed to be persuaded by his arguments and evidence. At the same time, these readings were amply utilized to educate ISL and, later, ISC members as well as many members of the IS (International Socialism, the organization that succeeded ISC).

Within this period, we need to single out the series of dramatic events that took place in 1956, some of which had a substantial impact on the American left. These events included the twentieth party congress of the Communist Party of the USSR in February, at which Khrushchev exposed many of the crimes committed by Stalin; the Hungarian Revolution in October and November; and the British, French, and Israeli invasion of Egypt in retaliation for

---

3 Hal Draper, "In Defense of the 'New Radicals'," *New Politics* IV, no 3 (Summer 1965), 5–28, https://www.unz.com/print/NewPolitics-1965q3-00005.

Nasser's nationalization of the Suez Canal at the end of October. The twentieth party congress and the Hungarian Revolution in particular had a great impact on the American Communist Party, at the time the U.S. left's largest and in many ways dominant organization. After losing in the early fifties a very large number of members, many of whom had been the direct victims of Senator McCarthy's witch-hunts, the CP also saw thousands of members who had withstood McCarthyism and remained loyal leave the organization in 1956 and shortly afterwards. The American Communist Party, which had now become little more than a rump, lost much of its hegemonic ideological and political role within the U.S. left, a hegemony that had been gained mostly during the years of the Popular Front that began in the mid-thirties and during the Soviet alliance with the U.S. and its allies during World War II.

While the former American Communists were generally repelled by the crimes of Stalin and the bureaucratic ossification of the regime over which he and his successors presided, this welcome reaction was not for the most part accompanied by a deeper structural understanding of the nature of the Soviet system and particularly of the great perils posed by the lack of democracy in a one-party state controlling the lion's share of political, economic, social, and cultural life. This helps to explain, for example, the sympathy that many of these former Communists expressed for Fidel Castro and Che Guevara, favorably contrasting their romantic, revolutionary, and apparently free-wheeling élan with the stodgy and conservative bureaucratic behavior of Cuba's Soviet partners. Unfortunately, most of the former American Communists were reluctant to look "under the hood" of this new Cuban vehicle, where they would surely have found an almost complete copy of the organizational and structural features of the Soviet state they had so much come to dislike. That is the main reason why they failed to distinguish the higher political popular *participation* in Cuban Communism from the quite different notion of *democratic control*, which was as absent in Cuba as in the USSR and the rest of the Soviet bloc. This attitude was particularly tragic in light of the fact that many of these former Communists and their children (several of whom I personally liked and politically worked with at Berkeley) played valuable roles as activists in the civil rights, student, and antiwar movements. Many of them were also to play an important role in the New Left and its principal organization, Students for a Democratic Society (SDS).

The other audience that Draper had to address was American liberalism and the small remnants of right-wing social democracy. Under Draper's editorship, *Labor Action*, together with its sister theoretical journal, *The New International*, had for years zeroed in on criticizing Americans for Democratic Action (ADA), the principal organization of American liberalism for its support for American cold war policies and accommodations to McCarthyism. The much less important but still significant right-wing social democracy also came under attack as in the notorious case of Sidney Hook, a former revolutionary Marxist who had turned apologist for McCarthyism, with his slogan of "Heresy Yes, Conspiracy No" and his conclusion that as a conspiracy American Communism had no right to exist and should not be tolerated.

In 1960, the organization Students for a Democratic Society was founded under the sponsorship of the League for Industrial Democracy (LID), a right-wing social democratic organization, and the United Auto Workers (UAW), at the time perhaps the most politically liberal American union. It did not take long before the obsessive anti-Communism of the UAW, and especially of the LID, would clash with the far less obsessive but soft-headed attitude toward the Soviet bloc prevailing in the brand new SDS as well as in most of the American left. These latter political currents tended to consider, for example, that *any* strong critique of, let alone opposition to, the Soviet bloc was politically suspect and came close to an apology for U.S. imperialism. At the same time, the liberal and right-wing social democratic anti-Communism was based in their open and even militant cold war support for the United States in the conflict with the Soviet bloc. However, there was an alternative perspective that did not really require a high degree of political and theoretical sophistication and should have been obvious to independent, radical democratic minds: to oppose both imperialisms, the Communist one led by Moscow and the capitalist one led by Washington, while supporting the self-determination of nations, be that nation Hungary in 1956 or Cuba in the early sixties. Unfortunately, this point of view was only held by a small minority of SDS members.

Once the SDS rejected and broke with the obsessive anti-Communism of their original liberal and right-wing social democratic sponsors, it remained for a few years a fairly open political organization that attracted an increasing number of radicalizing young people to its ranks. But under the impact of the growing and long-lasting U.S. imperialist attacks on Vietnam and Mao's Cultural Revolution in China that began in 1966, the SDS took a turn toward an increasingly pro-Stalinist politics. However, this time, that kind of politics did not take the form of sympathies with the USSR, a country that continued to be perceived as conservative and even headed toward the restoration of capitalism, but with Mao's China and its supposedly anti-bureaucratic politics, especially after the Cultural Revolution. However, it did not take long before the Maoist hegemony in SDS turned into Maoist political fragmentation and fratricide with the consequent disappearance of SDS by the beginning of the seventies.

The Articles in the *America as Overlord* Collection

Four of the articles in this collection are exclusively concerned with American and Western imperialism. Three of these deal with the U.S. imperial possessions in Okinawa, Samoa, and Guam. The fourth one is about the important Suez Canal crisis of 1956 when the Israeli, French, and British armed forces invaded Egypt, then under Nasser's nationalist leadership, because he dared to nationalize the Suez Canal. Besides repudiating the invasion of Egypt, Draper relates and analyzes why and how, in this instance, the US chose to act as the imperial arbiter, successfully pressuring the invading countries to withdraw their troops.

Three other articles also deal primarily with U.S. imperialism, but also take into account and analyze the role that the local Communist parties and the USSR played in these three situations. First, there is an article on Guatemala dealing with the CIA-organized invasion that overthrew the democratically elected government of Jacobo Arbenz in 1954, and the role of the local Communist party in that country. Second, there is also an article discussing Vietnamese revolts in the fifties and sixties organized and led by forces independent of North Vietnamese Communism, and their political potential as a democratic alternative for the Vietnamese people. Third, there is an article on John F. Kennedy's disastrous imperialist policies toward the Cuban revolutionary government led by Fidel Castro that came to a critical head during the CIA-organized invasion that was defeated by the Cubans in April of 1961. A recurring theme that unites these three different situations was Hal Draper's insistence that principled and militant opposition to U.S. imperialism should be accompanied by the development of a left-wing independent political posture on the part of revolutionary socialists. This was necessary in the imperial countries—to fight against any surrender of the right to national self-determination of the countries resisting imperialism that both metropolitan liberals and conservatives were likely to advocate. At the same time, in the colonial and subject countries, this kind of independent political stand was necessary so they would be able, when the occasion required it, to successfully prevail in any conflict with any victorious Communist movement that we knew, based on ample experience, would proceed to establish a one-party state suppressing independent unions and every other expression of democratic life, particularly those developing from below, let alone imprisoning those who opposed their new rule.

Behind Yalta

Particular attention should be paid to the first and last articles in this collection, which are also the two longest, that are truly exceptional in quality and played a major role in my own political education. The first article, well over fifty pages long, is titled "Behind Yalta: The Truth About the Second World War." This is an indispensable article for those who want to understand why World War II was fought and the origins of the cold war that lasted from the late forties until the collapse of the Soviet bloc in the late eighties and early nineties. Draper's account of the meeting that Stalin, Churchill, and Franklin D. Roosevelt held at Yalta in February of 1945, toward the end of World War II, and an earlier meeting of Churchill and Stalin in Moscow in October of 1944 show the cynical, Realpolitik content of those encounters in which by far the dominant topic on the agenda was how to divide the world among the victorious imperialist powers that would emerge with the defeat of fascism. When I read those descriptions, I could not help but draw a parallel with the legendary Mafia meetings to adjudicate jurisdictional disputes concerning the production and marketing of various illegal drugs and illegal union, loan sharking, and gambling rackets.

Draper's well-documented article and very rich historical account gives the lie, on one hand to the often-repeated Western ideological proclamation pretending that the Western powers fought World War II and the cold war against the Soviet bloc to defend freedom and democracy. On the other hand, it also gives the lie to Moscow's pretense to be a defender of Communism when it is clear that it assured the Western powers that it would not support any Communist takeover in Western Europe provided that the USSR be given a free hand in Eastern Europe. In particular, this was why Stalin withheld aid to the local Communists in the Greek Civil War in exchange for his getting the green light to take over Poland. Of course, those agreements at the end of World War II lasted no longer than the relation of forces among the contending powers that gave birth to them, a relatively unstable situation that gave birth to the almost forty-five years of the cold war.

These sorts of deals had nothing to do with FDR and the Democratic Party establishment being soft on Communism or any of the other slanderous legends spread by the American right about the cold war. Rather they were the outcome of a cynically well-calculated imperialist exchange. One reason why the American right wing had a certain degree of success in spreading such falsehoods was that most Americans simply did not know that at Yalta FDR was not only supposed to contain Stalin but also Churchill, who was trying to retain as much as he could of the British Empire, an intention opposed to the American imperialist perspective of opening the whole world to its interests and hegemony. In a few years, Churchill's designs were brought to naught by Indian independence and the anticolonial revolution, let alone Great Britain's clear subordination to American economic and political power. Once Britain had lost much of its power and became the closest ally of the United States by the 1950s, especially after Britain was put in its proper place by Eisenhower during the Suez Crisis of 1956, Americans could not understand why FDR had to play Stalin against Churchill. Again, it was Realpolitik and not any softness toward Communism that guided FDR's behavior at Yalta in 1945.

National Liberation

The last article in the collection, titled *The ABCs of National Liberation*, was perhaps of even greater importance in the political education of the members of the Berkeley ISC including myself. Although written as a pedagogical primer for young socialist students, it was not less brilliant and original in its analyses. As a political group that under the leadership of Hal Draper, the ISC was of course for the immediate withdrawal of US troops from Vietnam (as well as everywhere else for that matter). The issue also arose—as will almost inevitably arise in struggles for national liberation—of what attitude American revolutionary socialists should adopt toward the specific political groups that are leading the struggle in the countries subject to U.S. domination. This was a particularly vexing problem in the case of Vietnam in light of the great political power and influence exerted by Communist North Vietnam and the National Liberation Front (NLF), its South Vietnamese branch and ally, keeping in mind once again that as soon as they took power they would establish a top-down and thoroughly undemocratic one-party state (as indeed happened after the victory over the United States), thereby preventing the independent organization of workers and other oppressed groups.

That is why Hal Draper had shown a great deal of interest in the Buddhist-led revolts that occurred in Vietnam in the fifties and sixties in articles that are included in this collection. This political development in Vietnam should not be surprising since, as has happened in numerous cases elsewhere, authentic mass rebellions have often been organized by leaders whose ideologies have been framed in religious terms. However, the Vietnamese Tet offensive in 1968 demonstrated to Draper that the NLF had the overwhelming support (or at least acquiescence) of the great majority of the Vietnamese people, and that the Communist-led NLF was the only organized alternative left to defeat U.S. imperialism. In response to the new situation, Hal Draper came out in this document not only for the immediate withdrawal of U.S. troops (that was, of course, never in question) but also for a perspective favoring the military victory of the NLF while remaining opposed to its politics.

What I found especially valuable about this article was that Draper also presented a whole methodology to guide the ISC, and more broadly the left, on what stand to take regarding a variety of political situations involving not only national liberation movements but also international conflicts such as wars. Following the strategist Carl Von Clausewitz and the Marxist tradition, Draper defined this as the continuation of politics by other means. Draper's analyses in this article addressed such widely different cases as Ethiopia's resistance to Italian imperialism and the Spanish Civil War in the 1930s, the clash between China and Japan during World War II, the conflict between Stalin and Tito's Yugoslavia in the late forties and early fifties, the Algerian struggle for independence in the fifties and sixties, and the U.S.-sponsored invasion of Cuba in 1961.

Draper's approach is today very useful in understanding and reaching political conclusions based on a democratic and revolutionary socialist perspective regarding such diverse places and conflicts as Syria, Hong Kong, Iran, and especially Ukraine. These situations have become an important source of conflict with the widespread left political phenomenon of "campism," meaning the uncritical political support that many on the left give to any country or movement that opposes U.S. imperialism no matter how reactionary and antidemocratic that regime or movement might be.

Behind Yalta

The Truth About the Second World War

Introductory Note

The Second World War, according to the myth, was the Good War, the war "everybody" was for, the war that was really fought for democracy and civilization, and so on. The persistence of this myth has been due to one fact only: this war had the "best" enemy any war ever had, viz., a monster named Hitler. You need monsters in order to get several million people killed with equanimity. Still, inconvenient facts penetrate through people's consciousness every now and then.

On March 17, 1955, the New York Times *published a consciousness buster; at least that is what it could have been for anyone who read it. Not that it was inconspicuous. It was a thick sheaf of pages devoted to reprinting a bookful of documents that the Eisenhower State Department leaked to the* Times *after originally announcing it was not the time to release the documents officially. (The documents were officially released on December 29 of that year after a year long scandal rivaling that created by the later leak of the Pentagon Papers.)*

The State Department leaked this material over the objections of many, including the British prime minister, Winston Churchill, who, among other things, thought it unfair to his old comrades Stalin and Roosevelt who were not alive to defend themselves from misinterpretation.

All these acres of type were made public because of a campaign put on by the right wing of American politics to claim that Roosevelt and the Democrats had sold America out to the demonic Russians. The material proved the Democrats' innocence — and everyone's guilt.

The material presented here was published in Labor Action, *the weekly publication of the Independent Socialist League. The issue of* Labor Action *for April 4, 1955, was the only one we ever published that consisted exclusively of a single article, taking up all eight tabloid-sized pages. (Actually it was gotten up somewhat like a pamphlet.) As you will see, it did not confine itself exclusively to the new documents just issued; it matched the new accounts up with some that had been previously published — like Churchill's noted account of his deal in Moscow. The result is: the essay has been known to cause some thought even among people who think that the Second World War was fought simply to stop Hitler.*

To be sure, there was no intention of putting the whole story of the war into those eight pages. Among other things, a genuine history of the war would have to show, for example, how far the paladins of democracy (including and especially Roosevelt and Churchill) were from stopping Hitler as long as he was massacring only or mainly Jews, trade unionists, and antifascists; how thoroughly these democrats refused to do anything about the plight of the Jews under Hitler and after Hitler; up to and including the greatest war crime in the history of the world — the murder of two cities by order of a Missouri courthouse hack.

H. D.

Note on Sources

All quotations not otherwise ascribed are from the text of the Yalta papers as published by the N. Y. *Times* in a special supplement on March 17, 1955. For a history of the controversy surrounding the leaking of the papers see James Reston's columns, especially those of March 17 and December 30, 1955.

Titles of books cited are referred to, in this essay, in the following shorthand style:

Sherwood:
Robert Sherwood, *Roosevelt and Hopkins* (1948).

Churchill:
Winston Churchill, *Second World War,* vol. 6, *Triumph and Tragedy* (1953).

Leahy:
William D. Leahy, *I Was There* (1950).

Byrnes:
James F. Byrnes, *Speaking Frankly* (1947).

Stettinius:
Edw. R. Stettinius, *Roosevelt and the Russians* (1949).

Ciechanowski:
Jan Ciechanowski, *Defeat in Victory* (1947).

The battle over Yalta, which Secretary of State Dulles resignedly says he expects will go on "through the ages," is no mere accident of partisan factionalism. All the politics of the Allied camp in the world war was focused at the Yalta conference. It stands midway reflecting the politics of one war and pointing to the next.

The Tehran conference of the Big Three in 1943 had been an inconclusive preliminary to Yalta. After Yalta the Potsdam conference, coming later in 1945 saw the rounding out of the deal. But it was at Yalta — with the military victory in sight, and in sight also of the problems of the post war world — that the war aims of the Allied imperialist powers were concentrated into a few days of intense discussion and bargaining.

The fate of the world is in our hands, Churchill kept reminding his colleagues at the Yalta round table. "These are among the most important days that any of us shall live," he said at the 6th plenary session, expressing the thought not for the first time. Alone among the three Churchill, historian, gave tongue to a feeling of acting out a moment of historical destiny.

"It is a new picture the Yalta revelations gave us, a picture not of a treasonable sell out, but of an irresistible fate driving us down a blind alley," editorialized the Boston *Herald*.

By "irresistible fate" (inaccurate language) the editorialist means merely to convey his feelings of the impersonality and objectivity of that which, greater than the Great Men, drove the Yalta conference to its prepatterned end. He has the merit of realizing the triviality of trying to understand Yalta in personal terms of treason.

The liberals, worshippers in the cult of FDR, likewise scout talk of treason (as everyone above the level of a McCarthyite or an idiot must do), but only because they think inside a similar framework. For them, the important thing to prove is that Roosevelt and his entourage "honestly" sought Peace and Justice; of course, they made mistakes, but do we have the right to criticize them because we enjoy 20-20 hindsight? And anyway, they recall, Roosevelt was a sick man (and, strangest of all, some liberal friends of the Great Man have invented the baseless excuse that at Yalta he was sick not only physically).

Whereas to the troglodyte right wing the devil was Roosevelt and other traitors like Hiss, to the liberals the devil at Yalta is simply the bad, nasty, wicked Russian, who spoiled everything by failing to keep the promises he made, especially about Poland....

The full story of Yalta proves that this is a myth, not less silly than the GOP myth about treason.

There were no personal devils around the Yalta table — also no heroes, no saints, no knights, and no men of honor.

There were only three earthy imperialists, who, temporarily united for a military victory against the Axis, knew that the agenda read: *Who will get what ?*

One cannot begin to understand the record of Yalta or to read the recently published papers intelligently except on the background of the fierce and bitter conflicts *within the Allied camp,* over rival imperialist aims, jockeying for the upper hand in the coalition.

One of the big facts which explain Yalta is that the most intense antagonism was not between U.S.-Britain versus their Russian ally, but between the U.S. and Britain themselves!

The politics of the whole period, so different from today's, has to be recaptured — in order to see how the politics of today was born, the post-Yalta cold war of capitalism versus Stalinism.

The Yalta conference summed up one pattern of imperialist rivalry and gave birth to another.

The operational name given to the Yalta conference is the symbol. "I suggest `Argonaut'" wired Churchill to Roosevelt the preceding December, because of the Greek myth's association the Black Sea area. Roosevelt replied: "Your suggestion Argonaut is welcomed. You and I are direct descendants."

Direct descendants? Perhaps he thought he was going to find the Golden Fleece of world domination in Yalta. Neither of the direct descendants remembered that it is in the tale of the Argonauts that Jason sows the dragon's teeth, from which spring up armed men who turn against their creator, then rend each other to the last man.

1. The Dirty Word

"Imperialist" is a dirty word. At any rate some may think so, associating it with radical soap box speeches.

Before going into either the Yalta record or its background, let us get a good look at what imperialists look like, how they talk; more important, how they think. This chapter will be a series of exhibits .

What makes an imperialist mentality? At the very least, the habit of thinking in terms of the power of big and strong states over small nations and unbelligerent peoples; as hallmarks of imperialist thinking, surely no less can be said?

Leaving aside at this time any complicated ideas about the economic roots of the imperialist mentality, let us get acquainted with our three actors in the Yalta drama. You are not likely ever again to get so close an approximation of frank imperialist talk, when the realities have to be put on the table.

Another editor got a lively feeling from the record as he read it:

The records make it clear how much the three enjoyed having the fate of the world in their hands, to settle with a nod here, a set of initials there. . . . (Des Moines *Register.*)

Anyone who reads the papers can appreciate this appraisal. As a subjective statement it cannot be documented with quotations; it emerges from the whole. What it points to is not really any irresponsible feeling of glee about dangling the globe of the world on a fingertip; what it reflects is the obvious consciousness of overlordship that emanates from the record.

(1) The Big Three, said Churchill with comfortable good humor, was a "very exclusive club." According to *Byrnes*, he went on to remark that the entrance fee to this club was "at least five million soldiers or the equivalent."

Everyone has heard the apocryphal story about the remark that Stalin was supposed to have made in Yalta: "The Pope? How many divisions has *he* got?" It seems that Stalin never actually said exactly this, though the idea was there. But if the famous story is supposed to illustrate the military minded crudeness of the Moscow totalitarian, what shall we think of the democratic statesman?

Although apparently Stalin never applied the principle to the pope, he did put it in just such terms with respect to the issue of reparations for France. None for France, said the marshal. *"He said that he respected France but that he could not ignore the truth and that at the present moment France only had 8 divisions in the war"* while Tito had 12 and the Lublin Poles had 13. (2nd plenum.)

The "exclusive club" crack was directed by Churchill against France, for DeGaulle was sulking about being left out of Yalta. Contempt of nations even smaller than France filled the talk, and it is known that not all are yet public.

(2) Stalin was behind no one in the heavy handedness of his scorn for small nations that might pretend to have a say in the world. At a dinner meeting (February 5) he blurted out straight talk about the right of the three great powers to dominate.

> He said it was ridiculous to believe that Albania would have an equal voice with the three great powers who had won the war and were present at this dinner. He said some of the liberated countries seemed to believe that the great powers had shed their blood in order to liberate them and that they were now scolding these great powers for failure to take into consideration the rights of these small powers. Marshal Stalin said that he was prepared in concert with the U.S. and Great Britain to protect the rights of the small powers but that he would never agree to having any action of the great powers submitted to the judgment of the small powers.

> The President [Roosevelt] said he agreed that the great powers bore the greater responsibility and that the peace should be written by the three powers represented at this table.

Churchill, who is a statesman, demurred with some platitudes about the rights of small nations — specifically, the right of small nations to sound off in talk:

> The Prime Minister, referring to the rights of the small nations, gave a quotation which said: "The eagle should permit the small birds to sing and care not wherefore they sang."

It would be difficult to say whose remarks were more contemptuous of the "small birds."

But it is not recorded that Stalin repeated at Yalta the suggestion he had thrown out earlier, that the Allies invade Switzerland (in order to teach the Germans that they shouldn't have been such barbarians as to invade the Low Countries). The suggestion about invading Switzerland, "in order to outflank the Siegfried Line," was reported to Washington by General Deane, head of the U.S. Military Mission in Moscow, according to one of the documents in Vol. I of the Yalta papers. A leading Swiss paper has subsequently revealed that Roosevelt himself domineeringly demanded from the Swiss that they open up to Allied troops.

(3) There was a peculiar interlude at the 3rd plenary session. Speaking of the proposal for big power veto rights in the projected UN, Churchill approved and remarked:"The matter looks as though the three great powers are trying to rule the world," but (he went on) we're really trying to save the world.

At the reference to ruling the world, Stalin's ears pricked up suspiciously. "I would like to ask my friend Mr. Churchill to name which power might intend to dominate the world," he said. Not Britain, he was sure (he said); not the U.S.; that left the Soviet Union . . . Did Churchill perhaps hint — ?

> The Prime Minister replied that he had spoken of the three powers who could collectively place themselves so high over the others that the whole world would say these three desire to rule.

The tenseness passed. It seems it was only a question of whether three or one would rule. There were sensitive souls around.

(4) On another occasion, after Yalta, Stalin is again recorded as denouncing the reprehensible cheekiness of small nations. On Harry Hopkins' last mission to Moscow (May 1945), Stalin is recorded as charging that "after all two world wars had begun over small nations"! (Thus the "Marxist" Stalin.) There was a tendency by small nations, he complained, to create differences among the Great Powers. And "he was quite prepared to tell the little nations this to their faces." (*Sherwood*, P. 911.)

At this meeting, also, Stalin asked Hopkins what would be the good of Big Three agreements "if their decisions could be overturned by the votes of such countries as Honduras and Puerto Rico." (*Sherwood*, P.893-4.)

(5) Where Stalin inveighed, the democrats found amusement. Here are the democrats at a Foreign Ministers' session at Yalta (February 11). They are discussing invitations to the coming UN conference: *"It's good to have a Moslem or two,"* says Britain's Eden, and then he mentions that Roosevelt is due to have "a cup of coffee" with Ibn Saud after the conference.

Stettinius said he had no objections (to Moslem window dressing, that is), and Molotov muttered, "I don't know if Saudi Arabia will be much help." (But Old Leadbottom did know how much help Ibn Saud would be, *and* to whom; he knew that this mighty king was on the payroll of a couple of oil companies.)

Eden's gentlemanly snicker had popped out at a previous session. Stettinius mentioned that Ecuador had declared war, and the record reads: *"EDEN: laughed."* This is the sole passage in which Ecuador has the honor of appearing in the Yalta history. It will not make them happy in Quito.

(6) In another connection, at a plenary session, Roosevelt had to explain why certain Latin American states had not declared war. The State Department told them not to, he related (mistake by Sumner Welles, he claimed), but now they would be given the signal. . . . The dogs, apparently, were expected to jump through the hoop whenever you snapped your finger.

It was not only the Latin Americans who were expected to declare war to suit the convenience of the overlords.

In a message to Roosevelt about arrangements for sailing to Yalta, Churchill brought up the difficulty of getting warships through the Dardanelles and into the Black Sea, in view of the international conventions governing the Straits. *"One way would be for Turkey to declare war,"* he writes, opining that she would be "very willing".

However, it turned out that Turkey didn't have to declare war in order to solve the transportation problem. (Like the Latin Americans, however, she had to declare war shortly in order to get a membership ticket to the UN conference.)

(7) Perhaps this is the place to mention another note that was struck in the midst of the Yalta symphony of paternalistic overlordship, even though it refers to U.S. internal politics. The same smell will be noticed. At a dinner on February 10, Roosevelt told a little story. As recorded in the papers it is a flawless gem, the Lord talking about his flock:

He said he remembered when he first became President the United States was close to revolution because the people lacked food, clothing and shelter, but he had said, "If you elect me president I will give you these things," and since then there was little problem in regard to social disorder in the United States.

(Roosevelt told two other fairy tales at this same dinner.)

(8) With some exaggeration, but not too much, one might set out to prove that there was a positive competition among these three smug overlords as to who could be more overbearing and insulting about the rabble that didn't belong to the Exclusive Club. At the 6th plenary session, Stalin remarked that the Polish people were "still quarrelsome," though he also granted that they had produced some scientists and even mentioned the name of Copernicus, perhaps because the latter had no known anti-Soviet record.

Roosevelt hastened to agree that the Poles were "quarrelsome." In fact, he raised the ante. The Poles are a quarrelsome people "not only at home but abroad," he pointed out, as he pleaded for "some assurance for the 6 million Poles in the U.S." that there would be free elections in Poland.

Not to be outdone, Churchill shortly chimed in with *"I do not care much about Poles myself."* (Incidentally, contrary to the headlines, Churchill did *not* actually deny in Parliament that he had said this.)

However, while Churchill seemed to resent the fact that the Yalta papers exposed this indiscretion of his, he himself had done the same kindness for his good friend Roosevelt. In *Churchill,* vol. 6, he quotes FDR as saying at Yalta's first session, *"Poland has been a source of trouble for over five hundred years."*

Troublemakers, that's what these Poles are! Three times this nation was dismembered and partitioned by another Big Three (Germany, Austria, Russia) who in their own day were overlords of Europe; see all the trouble they made?

Moreover, after being partitioned, the Polish people never ceased fighting against the foreign rulers. ("This animal is wicked; it defends itself when attacked.")

During World War II itself, Poland was the one country occupied by the Nazis where not a single quisling was found; which maintained the biggest, most courageous underground resistance. Troublemaker! In short, quarrelsome.

Like master, like man. Harry Hopkins was FDR's alter ego, the Grey Eminence of the White House:

A friend of Harry Hopkins and mine [writes the then Polish ambassador to the U.S.] told me that on Harry's return from Moscow [June 1945] he had remonstrated with him for having agreed to conclude with Stalin "a deal so unfair to Poland." He quoted Harry Hopkins' reply: "After all, what does it matter? The Poles are like the Irish. They are never satisfied with anything, anyhow." (*Ciechanowski,* P.382-3.)

This comparison of the Poles with the Irish, by an Anglophile, was not accidental. The British always thought the Irish were a cantankerous lot. "This animal is wicked. . . ." It so happens that Engels too had once linked the Irish and the Polish, but with admiration for the national struggles.

(9) At this same plenary session, the question of a trusteeship system for the UN came up. It had barely been mentioned when Churchill exploded at the very idea that an impious finger might be laid on the British Empire. The Yalta notes taken by Matthews reflect the self-righteous anger of the democrat who had said that he had not become the king's first Minister in order to preside over the liquidation of the British Empire: "I will not have one scrap of the British Empire lost, after all we have done in the war," he expostulated.

I will not consent to a representative of the British Empire going to any conference where he will be placed in the dock and asked to defend ourselves. Never, never, never.

If you tell me that we are not to go and be brought up before a vague tribunal and be told how to be good and proper, I will not object.

Every scrap of territory over which the British flag flies is immune.

Stettinius calmed him down by assuring him that the U.S. plan for the trusteeship rigmarole would have no applicability to the British Empire or to any possession of the big powers — only Japanese mandates and such.

(10) It was also in connection with the British Empire, at this session, that Roosevelt indulged himself in a little joke at his pal Winston's expense — a mean joke.

The text of a Declaration on Liberated Europe was up for discussion. It contained a ritualistic reference to the Atlantic Charter and the right of all peoples to self determination. But Churchill apparently was in a deplorably suspicious state of mind about the purity of his colleagues' intentions.

Taking the floor, he said he was willing to agree to the draft "as long as it was clearly understood that the reference to the Atlantic Charter did not apply to the British Empire."

Then, quite contradictorily, he went on to refer to a Parliamentary statement of his to the effect that the principles of the Atlantic Charter were anyway already followed in the British Empire. "I sent a copy of this interpretation [statement] to Wendell Willkie," he concluded.

"Was that what killed him?" quipped Roosevelt. And the record reads "(Laughter)." We do not know whether Churchill laughed too.

A hilarious joke all around. The democratic signatories of the Atlantic Charter had not only exempted the British Empire from its sphere. In the May before Yalta, Churchill had announced in a public speech that it would not apply to defeated Germany. Roosevelt was making it clear that the U.S. was going to hold on to every possible Pacific island with no more of a by your leave than the Japanese had displayed in acquiring them.

In April 1944 a New York *Times* magazine article by Emery Reeves had ironically noted: "In the past few months we have been told that the Atlantic Charter does not apply to India, that it does not apply to Germany, nor to Poland, nor to the Baltic countries, nor to the Pacific — a strange remedy that cannot be given to the sick and may only be enjoyed by the healthy. . . ." (This sardonic Mr. Reeves was arguing that the Atlantic Charter had been a mistake to begin with!)

While on the subject of the Atlantic Charter, we must mention that, according to *Churchill,* Vol. 6, Roosevelt at Yalta expressed his happiness that the existence of the famous Charter was on the vague side. It seems that Roosevelt had mentioned the British Constitution and the fact that it did not really exist in writing:

> However [Roosevelt went on], an unwritten Constitution was better than a written one. It was like the Atlantic Charter; the document did not exist; yet all the world knew about it. . . . (*Churchill,* Vol. 6, P. 344.)

Churchill replied that "the Atlantic was not a law, but a star." And we all know how unattainable the latter objects are.

All in all, a delightful exchange between two eminent democrats.

(11) Churchill's imperialist instincts also steered him unerringly to immediate agreement with Stalin when the Russian dictator demanded three votes in the UN (by giving seats to the Ukrainian and White Russian constituent "republics"). Britain was going to have multiple votes for the dominions — "That is why, Mr. President," said Churchill at the Yalta session, "I have great sympathy with the Soviet request."

To Deputy Prime Minister Atlee back home, Churchill wrote from Yalta:

> That they should have two besides their chief is not much to ask, and we will be in a strong position, in my judgment, because we shall not be the only multiple voter in the field. (*Churchill*, vol. 6, P. 314.)

Tit for tat: such is the rule among imperialists when they are in a friendly mood for a swap. All that was being poured down the drain was unrealistic nonsense about the equality of nations. Overlordship was being institutionalized. Roosevelt was uneasy: how would he explain Russia's three votes to the naive people back home, who might even get "quarrelsome" about it? In preparation, he exacted a promise from Stalin and Churchill to support three votes for the U.S. if he, Roosevelt, proposed it.

As it turned out, American public opinion did heat up over the three vote deal. One reason, recalls Sherwood ruefully, was that "the State Department had been conducting an `educational' campaign intended to emphasize the absolute equality of the United Nations voting procedure which gave the little fellow exactly the same rights as the big ones."

But at the same time no one went for America's claiming three votes: it was dropped. The N. Y. *Herald Tribune* expressed what Sherwood calls the "healthy, intelligent attitude" in an editorial which said *inter alia*:

> Even as matters stand, the U.S. will be able to count on the sympathetic votes of the Philippines, Cuba and others quite as surely as the United Kingdom will be able to count on those of the dominions and almost as surely as the Soviets will be able to count on White Russia and the Ukraine. (*Sherwood*, P.877.)

So Roosevelt had his satellites who were "almost" as much under the U.S. dollar as the Ukraine was under Moscow's knout. The *Herald Tribune* understood the authentic atmosphere of Yalta.

(12) Now for an entirely different aspect of the imperialist mentality, not the least startling one.

One can understand the process of dehumanization of a soldier surrounded by blood and violence and immersed in the filth and muck of scenes of daily slaughter. Human beings, in extreme circumstances, can adapt to almost everything, even to living among hecatombs of dead. But side by side with this well known fact, American history presents an opposed ideal, that of the President who is reluctantly leading the war on behalf of principle but who is himself torn with compassion by the slaughter, for the slaughtered as well as the slaughterers, for the killing and the scenes of horror. . . . This is the image held of Lincoln in the Civil War.

At the opposite pole is the image of the savage ruler who exults in the blood of his slain enemies. It may seem an insinuation to ask where Roosevelt, a civilized president of the 20th century, fits in between these two types.

An incident at the Yalta conference was the second act of a little playlet whose first act had occurred at the Tehran conference. This Tehran story is related in Churchill's history; but essentially the same account is also given in another book which we prefer to quote.

This is the book by Polish Ambassador Ciechanowski, who tells about Mikolajczyk's visit to Washington in June 1944 (in- between Tehran and Yalta). Roosevelt himself was telling Mikolajczyk about Tehran:

> Then, with a note of playful irony, the President said that personally he had found no difficulty in adapting himself to Stalin's moods, and that he was pleased to say he appeared more readily to understand his specific sense of humor than "my poor friend Churchill," who did not seem to have much affinity with the Soviet dictator's personality.

> As an example the President, with visible relish, related an incident of the conference. When Stalin suddenly proposed a toast to the death of at least 50,000 German officers, the President said he immediately understood that Stalin meant German Junker militarists. But Churchill failed to grasp the jocular tone of Stalin's toast. He answered testily that

he could not drink such a toast "because Great Britain should never admit the killing of war prisoners." Stalin was visibly displeased. He gave Mr. Churchill what the President called a 'dirty look,' and the atmosphere between the British Prime Minister and Stalin became icy. [Churchill relates in his own book that he walked out of the room — H. D.] The President laughed heartily, saying that he saved the situation by suggesting "an amendment to Stalin's toast," and proposed a revised one "to the death in battle of forty-nine and a half thousand German officers."

The President said he was much amused when, during the Tehran conference, several incidents of this kind showed him the psychological difference between the Eastern chief, Stalin, and the "Victorian statesman, Churchill, who had kept a nineteenth century British mentality." (*Ciechanowski*, P. 292-3.)

In the background is an unspoken fact which changes the mood key from the macabre to the grisly. When Roosevelt was chuckling over this rollicking tale to his Polish visitor, the world had already been informed for over a year of the Katyn massacre — the deliberate mass slaughter of the officer corps of the Polish army, by the Russians, to make impossible the re-formation of an organized Polish resistance.

Washington scouted, or made out to scout, this charge as "Nazi propaganda" (just as, at one time, Roosevelt publicly denounced as Nazi propaganda any talk about Big Three quarrels, at a time when they were indeed pulling each other's hair out by the follicles). Perhaps Roosevelt really disbelieved it. It is to be doubted that Churchill was as naive. It is to be supposed that at least Churchill had no doubts as to the real meaning of Stalin's toast: it was something which the "Eastern chief" had already done, not to the Germans but to the Poles. . . .

This is the background for Act II of this particular drama, at Yalta. Roosevelt sought to continue his ingratiation with the "Eastern chief" by plucking on the string of *massacre*. And, incidentally, he also shows he was not so naive as to think that Stalin was merely having himself a peculiar jest. Here is Bohlen's account of the private talk with Stalin, February 4, the three of them alone:

The President said that he had been very much struck by the extent of German destruction in the Crimea and therefore he was more bloodthirsty in regard to the Germans than he had been a year ago. And he hoped that Marshal Stalin would again propose a toast to the execution of 50,000 officers of the German army.

(Note at this point, also, that Roosevelt says "execution," not "death in battle." He is not the fool he playfully acted in Washington. Or at any rate, by this time he knows what the Eastern chief likes to hear.)

Marshal Stalin replied that. . . . everyone was more bloodthirsty than they had been a year ago . . . He said the Germans were savages and seemed to hate with a sadistic hatred the creative work of human beings.

The President agreed with this.

Speaking of bloodthirstiness, especially bloodthirsty democrats, it may be in order to mention at this point that when Roosevelt's man Friday, Hopkins, visited Stalin in Moscow later, he told Stalin "he looked forward to what for him would be a pleasant spectacle, the present state of Berlin and he might even be able to find Hitler's body." (*Sherwood*, P. 912.)

Perhaps, the master had told the man how to chuck the Marshal under the chin. Thus Roosevelt amused himself with the "psychological difference" between the Eastern chief and the nineteenth century Victorian statesman who didn't like to hear cold blooded massacres being bandied about. Perhaps a future biographer will amuse himself with the "psychology" of this 20th-century capitalist democrat.

(13) But if the non-bloodthirsty Churchill was revolted by Stalin's yearnings for another Katyn massacre, it must not be supposed that delicacy of stomach was the only cause. As we will see when we analyze the politics of the inter-Allied imperialist struggle, the destruction of a living Germany in the heart of Europe (concomitant of the destruction of its officer corps) was a threat to British influence, which intended to base itself on its organization of the European Continent as against the American and Russian powers. Germany had to be defeated, yes, but Europe had to survive, and a Germany had to be at the heart of this Europe.

If this seems an unfair imputation against Churchill, in view of his civilized reaction to the Eastern chief, then let me turn to an episode which (as far as I know) is mentioned only in Admiral Leahy's book. Massacres, no: no one can take that away from Churchill; but it was not quite true that this true-born Englishman could not stand the very idea of killing war prisoners, provided it was on a selective scale.

At the 6th plenary session in Yalta, Leahy recounts:

The Prime Minister next presented the question of war criminals. He said that the "great war criminals" should be executed without formal trials. This would obviate any necessity for bringing them before a formal court, which he at that time considered unwise.

He insisted vigorously that traditional English practice would not permit trying before any British court any person accused of an offense that was not legally a crime at the time it was committed. (*Leahy*, P. 314-5.)

And so since British scruples would never stand for the injustice of such an unfair trial, why, shoot 'em without a trial! (Come to think about it, nineteenth-century Victorian statesmen were not always delicate about the lives of their enemies, either — for example, Indians and Irishmen.) As is known, Churchill later permitted himself to be convinced of the justice of the ex-post-facto newly-minted international justice of the Nuremberg trials.

(14) There is another interesting passage in the Yalta record (4th plenary session), this time between Churchill and Stalin in friendly agreement, the Victorian statesman's stomach having visibly firmed up by this time. The discussion came on the difficulties of moving Poland's western boundary deep into German territory so as "to stuff the Polish goose so full of German food that it got indigestion." Millions of Germans might have to be moved out of East Prussia and Silesia —

He [Churchill] said that he felt there was a considerable body of British public opinion that would be shocked if it were proposed to move large numbers of Germans, and although he personally would not be shocked he knew that the view existed in England.

STALIN: There will be no more Germans there, for when our troops come in the Germans run away and no Germans are left.

CHURCHILL: Then there is the problem of how to handle them [the runaways] in Germany. We have killed 6 or 7 million and probably will kill another million before the end of the war.

STALIN: One or two?

CHURCHILL: Oh, I am not proposing any limitation on them. So there should be room in Germany for some who will need to fill the vacancy. . .

It surely takes statesmen of caliber, Eastern chief and Western chief combined, to grasp the insight that killing an additional million on the battlefield would be handy for solving the frontier problem. Create enough corpses, and no one need worry about population crowding. Demographic experts will find the principle even handier in the era of the H-bomb, when population engineering is so much easier.

(15) There is an interesting series of scenes which can be collectively entitled "Public Opinion and the Imperialists."

Scene I is at a Yalta dinner meeting, February 5. The record reads:

Following a toast by the Prime Minister to the proletariat masses [sic] of the world, there was considerable discussion about the rights of people to govern themselves in relation to their leaders.

It was at this dinner that Vishinsky, in reply to a remark by Bohlen about American public opinion, "replied that the American people should learn to obey their leaders." Churchill, after toasting the proletariat, roared like a democratic lion: "although he was constantly being 'beaten up' as a reactionary," he said, he was the only one present who could be thrown out of office by democratic vote at any moment, and "personally he gloried in that danger."

With a fine sense of dramatic irony, Scene II opens on the same Churchill at the same dinner, after Stalin and Roosevelt had gone.

Churchill, Eden and Stettinius are left, discussing the UN voting system. Churchill says he's for the Russian view (the right of the big powers to veto small nation *discussion*) in order to ensure Big Three unity.

Eden takes "vigorous exception" and argues that this procedure would find no support in English public opinion. This doesn't faze Churchill: he is *"thinking of the realities of the international situation,"* he replies.

He does not say "Public opinion be damned." That comes in Scene III.

Scene III is a flashback about our democratic lion, back to another conference that prepared Yalta.

The previous October, Churchill had been in conference with Stalin in Moscow. (This was the Moscow conference which, we will see later, made the deal swapping Greece for East Europe.) Both Polish "governments," the London Poles and the Lublin Poles, were also present, for their country was on the bargaining counter.

In a private session, Churchill violently pressured the London Poles to accept the Curzon line as eastern boundary. Mikolajczyk, Romer and Grabski refused, even though Churchill shouted "There is no other alternative!"

Finally Grabski interposed with the assurance that Polish public opinion would never stand for it; no Polish parliament would ever accept it.

> "Well," answered Mr. Churchill ironically, "then there is nothing to prevent Poland from declaring war on Russia after she is deprived of the support of the Powers. *What is public opinion, after all? . . ."* (*Ciechanowski,*P.335.)

Scene IV, back at Yalta, shows character development in the plot, as a good drama should.

Stalin who, at Tehran had lectured Roosevelt that the way to overcome Americans' rejection of the Russian grab of the Baltic states was to subject them to a propaganda campaign, "was later to confess to Hopkins that [at Yalta] he became pretty fed up with hearing about American and British public opinion, believing that the President and the Prime Minister kept on referring to it merely as a device. . . ." (*Sherwood,* P.861.) But at Yalta, though fed up, he apparently decided that if democratic type demagogy meant to mouth phrases about public opinion back home, why, he could do it as well as the next man. So he did.

Thus we get the semihilarious passage (at the 3rd plenum) after Roosevelt and Churchill suggested that perhaps Stalin would be so "magnanimous" as to deviate from the Curzon line sufficiently to let Poland keep Lvov Province. Stalin rises in "indignation" to declaim that it was not Russians who originally fixed the Curzon line but Messrs. Curzon and Clemenceau, and "Should we then be less Russian than Curzon and Clemenceau? We could not then return to Moscow and face the people who would say Stalin and Molotov have been less sure defenders of Russian interest than Curzon and Clemenceau."

Finding that this went over like a house afire, Stalin got real interested in this new gimmick learned from his friends. Later, when he discussed with Roosevelt what Russia was going to grab in exchange for declaring war against Japan, he hauled it out again: the Supreme Soviet back home, he told FDR, would want to know what was in it for Russia and what was he going to tell them? His democratic friend took care of the problem, as everyone knows.

At Yalta Stalin was more in character at the dinner on February 10, when, apropos of French party strife —

The Prime Minister remarked that Marshal Stalin had a much easier political task since he had one party to deal with.

Marshal Stalin replied that experience had shown one party was of great convenience to a leader of a state.

(16) In a private Roosevelt-Stalin confab on February 8, the two Slaves of Public Opinion made the famous deal on the slices of Chinese territory which Moscow was to get for entering the Japanese war. Chiang Kai-shek was to be told about it ("consulted") later.

There was no ceremony on Roosevelt's part in trading another people's land for his own purposes: it has been sadly noted by his best friends that the president accepted all of Stalin's demands like a shot, without a single murmur. It was no skin off *his* class. (Yet to this day, some people pretend that "imperialism" is just a radical soapbox term.)

A not uninteresting sidelight is the fact that the Yalta agreement on this U.S.-Russian sellout of Chinese territory is explicitly based on nothing else than the "rights" of tsarist imperialism in the Russo-Japanese war of 1904. This piquant approach was officially taken by Stalin when he introduced his own draft of the agreement with:

> The former rights of Russia violated by the treacherous attack of Japan in 1904 should be restored, viz. . . . .

And *Sherwood* notes:

> It is quite clear that Roosevelt had been prepared even before the Tehran Conference in 1943 to agree to the legitimacy of most if not all of the Soviet claims in the Far East, for they involved the restoration of possessions and privileges taken by the Japanese from the Russians in the war of 1904.   (P. 866.)

In fact, in their February 8 conversation, Stalin based his demand for use of the manchurian railroads on the argument that "the tsars had use of the line. . . ."

Thus Stalin consciously presented himself as the continuator of tsarist Russian-imperialism — the imperialism for whose defeat Lenin had agitated in the war of 1904.

But when it came to Russian-national imperialism, Stalin had no monopoly. Just a couple of weeks before this, it happens, a Mr. Alexander Kerensky, anti-Bolshevik, had made a spirited public defense of all of Stalin's landgrabs, from the Baltic states to Bukovina, as being no violation of the Atlantic Charter. Stalin, Kerensky and Roosevelt found themselves in perfect accord with the tsar, and Yalta sealed it all.

Actually, the most important "exhibits" for this subject are in the chapters below. Here we have given some vignettes, allowing us to penetrate into the minds of the Big Three imperialists around the Yalta table.

2. Rift In the Loot

There are not many moments in history when we can do this. The realities of international politics are usually obscured by the cottony masses of highly moral platitudes that our rulers like to spout forth in their public acts — about justice and democracy and honor and peace and other such notions whose very existence is wraithlike when they get together around the table to divide the world.

At Yalta, of course, the imperialists of only one side were represented, Germany being the enemy. But for us who live in the cold war today, Yalta shows to us in action the rulers of both of the camps embattled in the present conflict. An Eisenhower for a Roosevelt, a Khrushchev for a Stalin, Churchill for Churchill — they are no different now.

On one subject the Big Three at Yalta were united, of course: war against the common enemy Germany. The Second World War was supposed to be a war against Nazism, against fascism, against aggression, against barbaric enemies of humanity and civilization.

It was nothing of the sort. It was a war against an imperialist rival by a hostile coalition of imperialist rivals, who in turn were torn by internal imperialist rivalries. The official war aims were belied by Yalta. The Big Three's deliberation's on Germany are all the proof one needs.

In the first place, of course, one of the participants was indeed that state which had helped to give the green light for the launching of the war in alliance with Hitler. Until he was attacked by his Nazi partner in plunder, Stalin had ravaged Poland and Finland hand-in-glove with the Hitlerites. The only one at Yalta who mentioned this embarrassing period was actually Stalin himself, defiantly flinging its memory into the teeth of his friends, said teeth being gritted but discreetly kept locked against reproaches.

Let bygones be bygones. Russia was now fighting the Nazi Beast, defending Civilization against Barbarism.

To ensure the postwar victory of Civilization, our civilized democrats at Yalta kept bringing up the question of — enslaving German workers as forced laborers for Stalinist Russia!

That would be proper punishment for those Nazi concentration camps. Who, by the way, were in those concentration camps? Why, German workers, of course; the Yalta democrats would teach the Germans a lesson by transferring them (not necessarily the same ones) to Russia.

The same German workers who had been the very first martyrs in the struggle against Nazism were going to be punished for the war started by Stalin's partner, by being enslaved to Hitler's partner.

It was *not* Stalin at Yalta who bought up the question of the enslavement of German workers. It was Roosevelt and Churchill who kept doing so.

The State department had been all prepared in expectation of the Russian demand for slave labor as part of reparations. In its Yalta Briefing Book (which, by the way, Roosevelt didn't bother to read, according to *Byrnes*) the State Department averred that "There is no compelling reason for the U.S. to oppose such claims within reasonable limits" — thus disposing of the moral bunkum to which the cold war has been compelling our imperialists lately — and especially recommended that Germans *who were not Nazis* ("politically passive") be ensured enslavement "with minimum standards of treatment and a relatively short period of service" as distinct from formerly active Nazis.

At the 2nd plenary session in Yalta, Roosevelt hastened to bring up the question of giving Russia "reparations in manpower," i.e., slave labor:

> First, there is the question of manpower. What does Russia want? The U.S. and British, I believe, do not want reparations in manpower.

The Russians said they weren't ready to discuss the question, and persisted in this answer throughout.

Hopkins passed a note over to Roosevelt, scribbling: "Could you ask him (1) Why not take all Gestapo Storm-troopers and other Nazi criminals. . . ."

But not even that distinction was made by the proposals repeated at Yalta.

Churchill phrased it as a callous deal, at the same session, in spite of the Russians' refusal even to take up the question:

> Our objective is seeing that Germany will not starve in helping the Soviet get all it can in manpower and factories and helping the British get all they can in exports to former German markets.

(See what the war was about?)

Roosevelt veered back to the subject once again in the session, referring to his desire to help Russia get "German manpower to reconstruct the devastated regions . . ." The Russians kept mum.

At the Foreign Ministers' meeting on February 7, Stettinius came back to it. He said the American delegation wanted "to know whether the subject of labor [in German reparations] would be discussed at the Crimean conference or at a later date." Molotov answered they were not ready to discuss it at Yalta, and the Americans' enthusiasm for filling Stalin's labor camps had to subside perforce.

Why were the Russians stalling on this at Yalta? *Leahy* writes only: "Since the Russians were using many thousands of prisoners in what was reported to be virtual slave camps, they had little to gain by discussing the matter." (P. 302.) That is, they didn't need a deal with the Moral Democrats on this; they were garnering their slave labor already, and at will.

(And incidentally they were very jealous about their supply channels too, namely, German troop surrenders. They howled bloody murder whenever they suspected that German troops facing their armies were trying to surrender not to them but to the Anglo-Americans. In his post-Yalta Moscow talks with Hopkins, in May 1945, Stalin, seeking an example of honest dealing by an American, chose to compliment Eisenhower's honesty in turning over to the tender mercies of the Russians some 135,000 German troops who had tried to surrender to the American army.)

Conversely, this also helps to explain why Roosevelt and Churchill were so anxious at Yalta to get the Russians to work out a slave labor reparations deal.

For, as we shall see, they wanted to restrain Russian demands on the German *economy*; the cheapest compensations they had to offer in exchange for going easy on German capital were the lives, labor and liberty of the German workers. Stalin knew that too, and refused to discuss slave labor at Yalta until he had first exacted the highest price he could on the rest of the German economic structure. That way he would get the most of both.

Certainly, of course, the Russians had thundered to the world their intention of exacting German forced labor; they did not suffer from moral scruples or bashfulness on the point. Our democrats did, however ("public opinion," you know), and Roosevelt's report to Congress drew a veil over this aspect of Yalta. But it was known, for the conference Protocol clearly referred to it. The N. Y. *Herald Tribune* at the time noted that the president was "a good deal more sensitive" than either Churchill or Stalin.

More sensitive? But of course. There *are* differences between democratic imperialists and totalitarian imperialists. . . .

If the Big Three's war had been a war in defense of democracy and the free world against Nazi aggression, as advertised, then whole scads of the Yalta record would be completely incomprehensible, as is indeed true for most readers. What, for example, could a naive but honest person make of the Yalta discussion on dismembering defeated Germany?

The nation that Hitler had oppressed was to be torn apart and tortured in punishment for the evil deeds of its tormenter; and thus the easiest way would be taken to laying the seeds of new war strivings by a German militarism that would surely be reborn. To defend democracy, a whole nation was to be ripped to pieces in the heart of Europe, and world democracy along with it. Even from a sane imperialist point of view, it was a mad scheme which could only take root even momentarily only in the minds of power-flushed imperialists.

But at the Yalta conference the Big Three rulers agreed on dismemberment. In the van was Roosevelt; in the rear, Churchill; but all went along.

Stalin brought the question up first, pressing for a definitive decision: all had agreed on it at Tehran, he said, but "the manner of dismemberment" was still to be decided. At Tehran, he recalled, Roosevelt had proposed cutting Germany into five parts; Churchill, two; he, Stalin, had agreed with Roosevelt.

Churchill said Britain agreed to dismemberment "in principle" but was undecided on details. Roosevelt repeated his stand in favor of dismemberment — "the division of Germany into five or seven states was a good idea." He proposed an agreement here and now.

Slow up, interposed Churchill, "we are dealing with the fate of 80 million people and that required more than 80 minutes to consider." This was Churchill's characteristic "statesmanlike" way of talking when he was not yet quite sure what he wanted.

A couple of months before Yalta, in fact, Churchill had raised the question with Roosevelt of "turning over parts of Germany to France after the collapse of Nazism" (Yalta papers, part I). At a Foreign Ministers' meeting in Yalta, February 7, Eden even mentioned "the assumption that Germany was to be broken up into individual states"!

But not long after Yalta, all parties concerned got less and less enthusiastic about dismembering Germany. Speaking to Hopkins in Moscow, May 1945, Stalin even pretended to "remember" that dismemberment had been turned down at Yalta! — in spite of the fact that the word "dismemberment" had been written into the surrender terms. Hopkins, surprised, protested that the U.S. was still for it.

No doubt Stalin's second thoughts were due to calculations as to whether Russia could expect to grab off more of Germany one way or the other. On Britain's part, reluctance about dismemberment hardened into opposition for general reasons which will be apparent shortly. In any case Churchill had speculated about a north-south partition, whereas the cold war brought about an even more artificial east-west division, even less viable for the German nation.

In the U.S., Secretary of the Treasury Morgenthau was pushing for a draconic and criminal plan to deindustrialize Germany and virtually transform it into an agrarian country. We can read in the Yalta papers that at first Churchill was "violently opposed" to the Morgenthau Plan, but came around:

> The proposal apparently appealed to the Prime Minister on the basis that Great Britain would thus acquire a lot of Germany's iron and steel markets and eliminate a dangerous competitor. (*Part I, Matthews memo* of September 20,1944.)

How helpful it would be if down-to-earth talk like this could be read sooner than ten years after the lying propaganda!

But at Yalta, it is obvious, Churchill (less so, Roosevelt) was still uncertain about what he wanted to do with Germany economically — milk it or use it for more grandiose plans to organize the Continent. The Russians did not need to have any hesitations. They came into Yalta with a detailed plan for a large-scale economic disemboweling and looting of Germany, under the head of reparations.

Maisky's report to the plenary session figured on Russia's taking a cool ten billion dollars of German national wealth, in *addition* to one billion dollars annually for ten years, to be paid in kind; eighty per cent of all German heavy industry was to be removed; one hundred per cent of all "specialized industry useful only for military purposes," this category including all aviation, synthetic oil, etc.

Stalin offered some of the loot to the U.S.: You don't want to take machine tools, he said, but how about helping yourself to some raw materials and "German property in the U.S."? — "The President expressed agreement with this view."

It was Churchill that kept throwing cold water on the scheme, without flatly opposing. He brought up "practical" difficulties as reasons for holding off decisions on any definite figure; he intimated that the twenty billion dollar total was high. But the course of discussion made it pretty plain what was concerning him.

Let it concern you too, dear reader, for here we get a long look into the economic problems of the imperialist war — not a full one, to be sure; not a rounded one, but it has the merit of being through the eyes of the imperialists themselves.

For Churchill and Roosevelt were anxious to push slave laborers on pal Joe, but when it came to disembowelling the capitalist economy of their enemy, they developed a maze of scruples, an access of qualms, and a fit of prudent responsibility.

"It was beyond the capacity of Germany to pay," objected Churchill. Taking reparations out of Germany's capital assets would "in turn make it more difficult for Germany to pay her bills," he added.

If Germany were made to pay for necessary imports, then "it would mean that the other countries would be paying for German reparations to those countries receiving them." Churchill said "he was haunted by the specter of a starving Germany" which would be a drag on the victors' economies.

Why not simply let them starve, these reprehensible Germans who had made the mistake of being exploited by Hitler? No, Churchill could not be as blithe as Stalin about that; for he knew that in the postwar world, facing a Russian Empire on one side and the American dollar colossus on the other, Britain's only hope would be to stand astride Europe; only as overlord of Europe could Britain hope to reach to the height of the Big Two; and it needed a Europe that was alive and viable, not broken and disembowelled; *therefore it needed such a Germany too.*

Furthermore, we have already quoted Churchill's remark about swapping slave labor to Russia in exchange for "former German markets" to Britain; but while the German economy had to be *subordinated* to British capitalism, it could not be made so poor as to be a charity dependent on its rich uncles. It was a fine problem in equilibrium for the victor-capitalists, in the last analysis insoluble; but Churchill and Roosevelt worried over some components of the problem.

"We lent Germany far more than we got after the last war," said Roosevelt. "That cannot happen again."

Churchill recalled an unexpected boomerang from reparations after World War I: "I remember we took over some old Atlantic liners [from Germany], which permitted Germany to build better new ones. I do not want to repeat that experience."

The State Department's Briefing Book for Yalta had made a related analysis, remarking on an unexpected effect of reparations on the world capitalist market: A one way flow of reparations from Germany "must necessarily interfere with the export trade of other countries. [In the first place, the U.S.!] The longer reparation lasts, moreover, the more strongly is Germany likely to become entrenched in the markets of the claimant states. . . ." (That is, German goods, sent in reparations, would wind up by capturing the foreign market of the receiver.)

These, considerations for the U.S. and Britain, were no consideration for Russian Stalinism, precisely because the latter's exploiting social system was not a *capitalist* type of exploitation.

Over the question of reparations — i.e., the economic future of defeated Germany — the two opposed camps which would soon square off against each other in our cold war took up their respective stances: rehabilitation of German capitalism, together with the same militarists and even profascists who had brought Hitler to power (the Western capitalist camp) versus the Russians' calculated effort to replace the weakened capitalist class of Germany with their own exploitative society of bureaucratic collectivism.

This is where we come in: here is the root of our world today.

Against the sole progressive force that could have offered a social alternative to both reactionary roads, the socialist working class of Germany, both imperialist camps combined with vicious suppression. The anxiety which Roosevelt and Churchill displayed to pay off Russia with German slave labor was capable of solving more than one problem for them! One of the things which kept the democratic Two convinced of Stalin's friendly bona-fides was the confidence they had in him that he too would not hesitate to crush any genuine workers' revolution in blood.

3. The Secret War

So far Yalta has permitted a deep glimpse into the imperialist springs of the warring powers, but we have not yet gotten close to the question which has been agitating American politics: Why did Roosevelt "capitulate" to Stalin? In fact, *was* there a "capitulation" to Stalin? etc.

One reason why this current discussion will remain fruitless "through the ages" as long as it remains on the present plane is that both the liberal and McCarthy-Knowland myth-makers bat each other about on the basis of a common assumption: the problem at Yalta was how the U.S. would handle

Russia. This is completely false. Nothing will ever be understood about Yalta or the politics of the Second World War as long as this is the conception of what Roosevelt was trying to do.

The United States did not see the lineup this way. Its major preoccupation was the bitter struggle with Britain, for imperialist dominance in the postwar world.

Fundamental to Yalta was *the primacy of the American-British antagonism*. We will begin to trace this in the present chapter, and we will see later how it tied in with the approach of both of them to the Russian rival.

This fact is not really open to dispute for anyone who bothers to go back and immerse himself in the political issues of the pre-Yalta war era — which now seems like a past geological epoch.

Sherwood, for example, notes that on the eve of Yalta the Grand Alliance "was beginning to show signs of cracking," and he truly adds: "and the first evidences of rupture at this time were not between the Soviet Union and the Western Allies, but between Great Britain and the United States. . . ." (P. 836.)

Why was this the primary antagonism, and how was it fought out during the war?

We have to be brief here about the basic background. American imperialism, fledged in early adventures like the Spanish-American War, emerged out of the First World War as a world creditor and a world power, feeling its oats, while the British Empire had already begun its decline and the Russian Revolution had stimulated the beginning of the end of colonialism. In the interwar period, the specific character of American imperialism crystallized. Relying on its overwhelming economic power and wealth to penetrate the world's markets and dominate its sources of trade and raw materials, the U.S. would only have been hampered by old-style colonialist methods which depended on political control and military force, characteristic of the British Empire.

The burgeoning imperialism of the U.S. needed only "independent" governments that would be reliable satellites primarily because of economic dependence, not because of the big stick (with only a judicious and limited use of the latter now and then, as recently in Guatemala or whenever necessary).

In general, therefore, it was in the interest of U.S. imperialism to have "open doors" in the world, rather than colonial areas which were closed off to its economic penetration by political restrictions imposed from London or Paris. This, incidentally, is the origin of America's original reputation as an "anticolonialist" power, a reputation now justifiably shot to pieces by Washington's role once it fully achieved its present dominant position as overlord of the whole capitalist world.

But this was also the origin of the irreparable clash between U.S. imperialism and British imperialism, whose curves were going in different directions. Today this question has been settled, and Britain "knows its place"; but during the Second World War against Germany, *this* war was also going on.

U.S. power threatened to undermine the British in every corner of the globe. Even Australia was fast becoming an economic satellite of the U.S., while formally remaining within the British dominion structure, and Canada was an older story. Everywhere, in the guise of the war emergency, or really because of it, the U.S. got economic footholds in British preserves — in Saudi Arabia, America's first toehold into the British Near East oil reservation; in East India oil and Dutch Guiana bauxite; in Argentina and other Latin American enclaves of British economic influence; in bases on Bermuda and other British Atlantic islands; in India and Malaya; in Hong Kong and Singapore; in Iran. The U.S. was also moving into the French Empire (Indochina, Dakar, Martinique, etc.). It was displacing Britain as the leading merchant marine power. It counterposed the Hull policy of "free trade" to British Empire restrictions.

But Britain could still expect at least to dominate the Continent, couldn't it? No, U.S. influence reached out to challenge London even there, and thwart its aims and aspirations. This sector of the British-American war-behind-the-war crystallized especially around the second front issue and the policy toward France and de Gaulle (to be explained). Even by 1943 the situation was getting almost too bitter to be kept in hand behind the scenes.

It spilled over at the October 1943 conference of the Big Three Foreign Ministers at Moscow:

> I ran into Harry Hopkins a few days later and he . . . hinted that Britain and America had not succeeded in appearing entirely united in Moscow, and that from Eden's attitude the Soviets might have concluded that Britain was trying "to ease America out of European problems." This struck me as an interesting comment from the lips of a man so close and friendly to Britain. (*Ciechanowski,* P. 229-30.)

The British-American antagonism was one of the axes of the second front controversy. The issue was: where?

What Russia demanded was not only a second front, but specifically a second front in Western Europe. What Churchill wanted was invasion through "the soft underbelly of Europe" in the Balkans.

The issue was not military-technical. What was at stake was the postwar constellation of power in Europe. We explained a couple of months *before* Yalta:

> The question as to where to invade Europe involved almost automatically the question of the domination of Europe after the war. The defeat of Germany through an invasion of Western Europe meant certain Russian domination of Poland, the Balkans, Finland, and a strong voice throughout the Continent. The latter was made all the more certain by the role of the Communists in the underground movements of Europe. Such a termination of the war would leave Moscow the `boss' of Europe with the exception of the Atlantic fringe of British satellites. (*New International,* December 1944, P. 305.)

But the U.S. threw itself into the scales against the Churchill view and in favor of the Russian version of the second front. This was not because of simple stupidity or "treason." *The Americans feared the domination of Europe not by the Russians but by the British.* This is the simple big fact which explains Yalta.

The typical American attitude of the time can be read in Wendell Willkie's book, *One World* (1943). The Big Three alliance, he believes, is too tightly controlled by the U.S. and Britain; Britain ought to be put in her place; her empire is far in excess of her needs; the U.S. ought to use Russia, which has been relegated to a minor seat, as a counterweight against overweening British presumption. . . . In the months just before Yalta, this general sharpening conflict took on acute forms that burst out in public scandals, as our quotation from *Sherwood* about the crack-up indicated. The immediate foci of the war-within-the-war were Belgium, Italy and Greece.

In all three countries Britain was engaged in intervening on behalf of reactionary political forces to ensure her own domination. In Belgium, the British sent in troops to smash popular demonstrations against the imposition of the Pierlot government, the representative of the Belgian big business collaborationists and the Société Générale du Belgique (one of Europe's biggest cartels, which worked with the Nazis). Pierlot had now sold himself to the British, and Churchill was determined to shove him down the throats of the Belgian people with bayonets.

In Italy, Britain twisted arms to oust Count Sforza as premier. Sforza was a liberal, none too leftish at that, who was however critical of the British and opposed to the monarchy. Sforza announced publicly that Churchill had insisted that he "accept King Victor Emmanuel III regardless of his heavy responsibilities with fascism," and he resigned under the pressure.

In Greece, as we will recount later in its place, British troops had invaded to crush the native national liberation movement, anticipate the arrival of Russian "liberating" troops, impose King George and puppet premier Papandreou to head a pro-British quisling regime.

Into this triple tinderbox in Europe, American imperialism deliberately threw a match. In a public statement which reverberated through Europe, Stettinius dissociated the U.S. specifically and sharply from the strong-arming of Sforza and Italy by Britain, and then added a rabbit punch: *"This policy would apply in an even more pronounced degree with regard to governments of the United Nations in their liberated territories."* Everybody knew this meant Italy and especially Greece.

Right on the eve of Yalta, the U.S. was deliberately challenging the influence of Britain over the Continent itself, in the public eye of all Europe!

Churchill cabled Roosevelt in a violent outburst of rage. His high-pitched screams were heard across the Atlantic. British-American relations were explosive.

Throw in another angle at this point: In the Lend Lease contract with Britain, Article VII referred generally to an economic *quid pro quo* in exchange for American aid. It was worded very vaguely and nothing had been done about it. In 1944 (suddenly or not so suddenly) State Department officials began to raise the question of pressing Britain for economic concessions, i.e., lifting Empire economic restrictions on British preserves in favor of American interests.

A memo in Part I of the Yalta papers (dated September 20, 1944) remarks that Treasury officials were pessimistic about what could be gotten from Britain "but they felt that at least it gave us a foot in the door" of the British commercial system. We learn also that the secretary of state was "shocked" to learn that Roosevelt had never put the arm on Churchill to get something out of Article VII. In other words, State Department wanted to call in the IOU, in addition to everything else boiling up.

Let us anticipate a little now and mention that *at Yalta itself* Stettinius sent a memo to FDR to get onto this job. Churchill thinks you are not interested in this subject, he memoed, and this "has tended to encourage the British to take an unyielding attitude on the matter of their Empire preferences and trade barriers." (What could be blunter?) Roosevelt handed Churchill a "Dear Winston" note dated February 10 demanding action toward "implementation of Article VII." (The rich top-hatted suitor twirled his black mustache and called in the mortgage on the penniless rival for his dearly beloved.)

In October before Yalta, as we have mentioned, Churchill had gone on safari to Moscow to bag a deal on Greece and East Europe. Roosevelt could not let this get-together of the other two-thirds of the Big Three pass without a cautionary warning. Five days before Churchill arrived in Moscow, Roosevelt wired Stalin:

> You naturally understand that in this global war there is literally no question, political or military in which the U.S. is not interested. I am firmly convinced that the three of us, and only the three of us, can find the solution to the still unresolved questions.

In this definitive statement of the extension of American imperialist interests to every corner of the globe, the words "only the *three* of us" meant "*not you and Churchill* by a private deal of your own." Roosevelt was declaring himself in on every British deal.

Churchill and Stalin made their deal in Moscow, and it would seem from a State Department paper dated as late as January 18, 1945, that American sources were still trying to piece the details of it together; at any rate, it frowned on this arrangement or any such arrangement. The U.S. wanted to keep the situation from jelling into spheres of influence controlled by either of its European partners; it wanted to handle spheres of influence through the UN where it had the upper hand.

Furious though he was, especially at the Stettinius statement, Churchill knew that to counter Russia he *had* to line the United States up on his side. To this end, preparing for the Big Three conference, he tried to get Roosevelt to "caucus" with him in advance.

This is the meaning of the series of appeals, which we can read in the Yalta papers, in which Churchill insisted that Roosevelt come for a preliminary conference with the British at Malta. "I beg you to consider this," he pleaded at one point at the cost of his dignity.

He struck the Cassandra key: "This may well be a fateful conference; coming at a moment when the great Allies are so divided and the shadow of the war lengthens out before us. At the present time I think the end of this war may well prove to be more disappointing than was the last." (January 8.)

Roosevelt kept fobbing him off; the last thing he wanted to do was to give "Uncle Joe" the idea that he was ganging up with Churchill at Yalta! But he finally reluctantly yielded. Churchill replied gratefully, "Pray forgive my pertinacity."

However, Roosevelt himself was going to show up only at the tail of the Malta conference; the combined Chiefs of Staff would be getting together there, and Eden and Stettinius would "run over the agenda."

About the Malta conference, *Sherwood* writes:

The Combined Chiefs of Staff had been meeting at Malta — and had been engaged in the most violent disagreements and disputes of the entire war. (One can read the official minutes of these meetings without suspecting that a harsh word had been exchanged, but some of those who were present tell a much more colorful story of what went on.) (P. 848.)

What was this fierce battle about? *Sherwood* vaguely indicates a military disagreement over strategic plans for the drive to Berlin, something like the disagreement that Eisenhower explains in *Crusade for Europe* for this period. It is hard for this nonmilitary outsider to see why this debate should have been so violent. But *Leahy* (P. 294) gives an entirely different explanation of the "acrimonious sessions" at Malta. According to him, the British were pressing for a Mediterranean attack in addition to the Western front, and he calls it a long-standing difference, indicating that it was the old issue of the second front all over again in a new form.

This makes better sense; and it is a fact that *Leahy* is less diplomatic about suppressing inconvenient facts than Eisenhower is in his book. If Leahy is right, then the issue was properly a bundle of dynamite just before Yalta and while the British invasion of Greece was still going on. The British were proposing a last joint effort to halt the threatened Russian domination of the Continent, as it would be jelled by the military disposition of forces in conjunction with the political.

Stettinius reports an after-dinner conversation with Churchill at Malta, before Roosevelt arrived for the hail-and-farewell:

> During the course of the conversation Churchill expressed utter dismay at the outlook of the world. . . . It was his opinion that future peace, stability, and progress depended on Great Britain and the U.S. remaining in close harmony at all times. (P. 67.)

But this bid by Churchill for a united U.S.-British front against Russia at Yalta got nowhere.

Even leaving aside the big questions at Yalta, for the moment, Roosevelt's behavior at the conference dramatized his thought-out strategy for world politics, which was closer to Willkie's conception than to Churchill's. This is true even on the personal level.

At his first private talk with Stalin at Yalta (February 4), Roosevelt took every opportunity, big and little, to knife Churchill in the back. He especially wanted Stalin to know that he was wielding the knife. Here is a passage in the key of the backstairs gossiper:

"The President said he would now tell the Marshal something indiscreet, since he would not wish to say it in front of Prime Minister Churchill. . . ." (It is a crack at Britain's de Gaulle policy.)

Discussing a possible surplus ship deal with Stalin in another private talk, Roosevelt threw in the following clod of mud: "He said that the British had never sold anything without commercial interest but that he had different ideas."

It was in this talk too that Roosevelt said he'd like Britain to give Hong Kong back to China for an international free port (i.e., wide open to the U.S.). "He said he knew Mr. Churchill would have strong objections to this suggestion." (He knew, of course, that Mr. Churchill would go through the ceiling.)

More: He felt (Roosevelt told Stalin) that Britain should not take part in the trusteeship over Korea "but he felt that they might resent this." Stalin opined that Churchill might "kill us" and urged letting the British in.

Throwing a dart also in the direction of France, FDR complained to Stalin that Britain wanted to give Indochina back to France.

As one reads these goings-on by Roosevelt at Yalta, it is not his moral character which impresses one, but his consistent carrying out (up to and including mere backbiting) of the strategy of ostentatiously divorcing himself from Britain with relation to Stalin.

But as long as we have mentioned his moral character, we cannot help quoting a remark in his sycophant Robert Sherwood's book, where Roosevelt is constantly represented as a dear friend of his chum Winston. Writing about Roosevelt's Fourth Inaugural Address just before Yalta, Sherwood worshipfully notes that Roosevelt said: "We have learned the simple truth, as Emerson said, that `the only way to have a friend is to be one.'" And Sherwood comments: "I had the feeling that he was summing up his most profound beliefs. . . ." (P. 846.)

4. Kindness and Kings

The primary British-American antagonism lay behind Yalta's consideration of a number of countries. The references to France at Yalta, and indeed all Allied politics with regard to France, can be understood only within this framework.

From the beginning Britain took de Gaulle under its wing, as the British channel for the (hoped-for) domination of France and the Continent. Washington, on the other hand, continued to recognize Vichy as the legitimate government of France, and kept this up as long as possible.

Until well into 1944 Roosevelt insisted on regarding de Gaulle as simply an adjunct to Britain's forces, without according him recognition as representing "France." This stand naturally enabled the Americans to demagogically play the democrats at first by insisting that France had no political voice until the French people could freely elect one.

It is for this reason, seeking a counterweight to Britain's De Gaulle, that Roosevelt went in for the reactionary game of recognizing the Giraud-Darlan profascists, Vichyite turncoats, in French North Africa — though the stench that this produced forced him to duck out.

In connection with this tug-of-war over the prostrate body of France, Eisenhower has a tale to tattle on Roosevelt, in his *Crusade for Europe,* as he relates his conversations with Roosevelt in Casablanca in 1943:

He [Roosevelt] speculated at length on the possibility of France's regaining her ancient position of prestige and power in Europe and on this point was very pessimistic. As a consequence, his mind was wrestling with the questions of methods for controlling certain strategic points in the French Empire which he felt that the country might no longer be able to hold. (P. 136.)

For Eisenhower, this is a remarkably forthright way of stating that Roosevelt was plotting how to take over the French Empire. No doubt!

The circumspect Eisenhower twists the knife on his next page, even indicating documentary evidence in a footnote to validate his accusation:

I found that the President, in his consideration of current African problems, did not always distinguish clearly between the military occupation of enemy territory and the situation in which we found ourselves in North Africa. He constantly referred to plans and proposals affecting the local population, the French army, and governmental officials in terms of orders, instructions and compulsion. It was necessary to remind him . . . that, far from governing a conquered country, we were attempting only to force a gradual widening of the base of government, with the final objective of turning all internal affairs over to popular control. He, of course, agreed . . . but he nevertheless continued, perhaps subconsciously, to discuss local problems from the viewpoint of a conqueror.

Roosevelt certainly was in a hurry to take over. This is the background for his attitude on France in connection with Yalta.

Thus, in the above-mentioned private talk with Stalin where Roosevelt wanted to tell him "something indiscreet," the carefully planned indiscretion was the statement —

. . . that the British for two years have had the idea of artificially building up France into a strong power which would have two hundred thousand troops on the eastern border of France to hold the line for the period required to assemble a strong British army. He said the British were a peculiar people and wished to have their cake and eat it too.

Roosevelt on the contrary only wanted to eat, to tear down France into minor vassalage so as to reduce Britain's counter-strength and subordinate both to the Big One. He knew that Stalin would not object to vacuums created in Europe.

We have already mentioned Roosevelt's idea of disengaging France's claw on Indochina, mentioned to Stalin in one of the private confabs. At his meeting with the U.S. delegation on February 4, Roosevelt also mentioned that "He had no objection to any U.S. action . . . in Indochina as long as it did not involve any alignments with the French."

In one seance with Stalin, Roosevelt laughed at de Gaulle's penchant for comparing himself with Joan of Arc. At the plenary sessions Churchill persisted in hammering for giving France an occupation zone of its own in Germany, plus membership on the Control Commission. At first Roosevelt would go along only with the first part. When Stalin privately asked him why even that much, Roosevelt answered "it was only out of kindness." Stalin and Molotov vigorously agreed. (Incidentally, *Byrnes*, whether by simple mistake or out of diplomacy, ascribes this remark about kindness to Molotov!) But before the conference closed Roosevelt conceded the rest of the proposition to Churchill, and Stalin thereupon immediately assented too.

Roosevelt's drive for a weak France on an atomized continent is an integral part of the world strategy that produced Yalta. So kind, so good, so pure.

The conference is drawing to a close. The overlords of the world are at dinner:

Marshal Stalin then said he thought more time was needed to consider and finish the business of the conference.

The President answered that he had three kings waiting for him in the Near East, including Ibn Saud.

We would like to write stage directions for this dialogue. "I've got three kings waiting for me," he says over the soup course, and rolls it on his tongue. Not necessarily in snobbishness or vainglory; just properly conscious of an overlord's power. The words should not be read off with special emphasis; they must be tossed out casually, as if saying, "Sorry, can't stay, I've got to catch a train."

The three kings in his hand, with whom he had to deal, were Ibn Saud of Arabia, Haile Selassie of Ethiopia and Farouk of Egypt. Another side of this tale was later told by Hopkins. Roosevelt had dropped the "three kings" on the table before a dinner tableful. Churchill had to rein in his curiosity and suspicion.

"Later that night," Hopkins narrates, "he, Churchill, sought me out, greatly disturbed and wanted to know what ere the President's intentions in relation to these three sovereigns." Hopkins assured the worried prime minister that it was just "a lot of horseplay," social stuff.

> Nothing I said, however, was comforting to Churchill because he thought we had some deep-laid plot to undermine the British Empire in these areas. The next day the Prime Minister told the President that he was also going into Egypt after a brief visit to Greece and see each of these sovereigns himself, and had already sent the messages asking them to remain in Egypt for conferences with him immediately after the President had left. (*Sherwood*, P. 871.)

The aura that surrounds this incident, more amusing than important though it is, tells more about politics at Yalta than yards of published commentary.

What was Churchill so worried about, that he trailed in a royal flush after Roosevelt and the three kings? Plenty. Ethiopia was the least important, but it is worth mentioning that during the war Britain was making valiant efforts to separate the Negus from some of his territory, in favor of adjoining British Somaliland. He could do without Roosevelt getting into *that* friendly game.

Britain's apprehensions about Egypt, of course, are apparent in view of subsequent history.

As for Ibn Saud, here was the most acute danger. Early in 1944 the American government had negotiated a deal: twenty-five million dollars to Saudi Arabia for oil concessions to be turned over to Standard Oil and Texas Oil; the U.S. to spend one hundred million dollars to build a pipeline for the companies; finally, the U.S. to buy the oil at a price higher than oil on the domestic market. Where did this leave Britain in the area which had once been its stamping-ground?

Churchill, vol. 6, tell a story that must be heartrending to all Churchillian true-born Englishmen, if understood in this context. It seems on the surface to be only a bit of Eastern color.

When Ibn Saud came aboard Churchill's ship, he came bearing gifts to Churchill's party — magnificent perfumes and gems, costly robes, etc. Churchill had prepared gifts in return but he unexpectedly found himself so outclassed that he told the king that the real gift was going to be a superdeluxe bulletproof auto. Churchill explains that the Arab gifts, turned in by all the Englishmen to the Treasury, later paid for the special auto. We need hardly add that no member of Churchill's entourage was unaware of the financial source of the expensive baubles that Ibn Saud was regally handing out to the ex-imperialist overlords of the area, as if to say, "Can *you* top this — you who have come trailing after Roosevelt?"

Time heals all. Churchill's memoirs do not hint at the gall that rises in the throat and chokes. It was a fitting epilogue to Yalta.

The smell of oil hung over Yalta in another connection — Iran. Here there was a three-way conflict, though it had begun as a part of the British-American war.

The British had long dominated Iranian Oil, but the American "foot in the door" was moving in. A large number of American advisers to the government were at large in the country: Millspaugh as administrator-general of Finance; A. B. Black for agrarian reform; Major-General Ridley plus an officer staff for the Iranian army; and many others who were doing London no good.

Over a year before Yalta, Socony-Standard and Vacuum (American) and Shell (British) had both tried to get the Iranian government to give them concessions along the Afghan and Baluchistan borders. The cabinet, under nationalist pressure, refused, or anyway refused to choose, although the premier favored a grant to one or the other.

Then the Russians decided to deal themselves in (all three allies had troops in the country). The Iranian government said: No concessions to anyone until later. Russia started a campaign of pressure to get the northern oil fields; the Russian press denounced the government violently; pro-Stalinist demonstrations were organized in Iran; Moscow's Vice-Commissar of Foreign Affairs Kavtaradze threatened and stormed. The cabinet resigned in the crisis, under pressure.

Among the Yalta papers is the report to Washington by Harriman, ambassador in Moscow, made only three weeks before the conference and thought important enough to be immediately put on Roosevelt's desk for his personal perusal. Harriman described the Russian pressure on Iran and ominously mentioned: "At the height of the controversy *Izvestia* asserted that there was no legal basis for the presence of American troops in Iran." After the fall of the cabinet, he concluded, the pressure from the Kremlin relaxed "but the Soviets made it clear that they did not intend to drop the issue."

Iran was one question on which Eden succeeded in caucusing with Stettinius at the Malta preconference. In this case, in the face of the Russian push, the Americans did agree to make a united front. The idea was to get Russian agreement on postponing all oil concessions in Iran until after the war.

It never came to a head at Yalta because, at the Foreign Ministers' sessions, Molotov made it clear no agreement was possible.

At the February 8 session Eden inaugurated the question: The Iranian government should be master in its own house, *"otherwise the Allies might find themselves in competition in Iranian affairs."* The British had no wish to veto oil concessions for Russia, if and when; Stettinius chimed in with the same reassurance. Molotov gave no ground: Russia still wanted to "persuade" Iran to change its mind; but he did say that "the situation was not acute at the present time." In the course of talking, the record shows, he also said "Kavtaradze had returned and the strong-arm methods he had used have subsided."

But two days later, when Eden and Stettinius tried to get him to join in any kind of communiqué on Iran, Molotov did his "bump on a log" act: *No, nothing to add. . . . No, no communiqué. . . . No, no reference to Iran whatsoever in any release. . . .* The next day at luncheon Stalin made a swipe at Iran: "any nation which kept its oil in the ground and would not let it be exploited was, in fact, `working against peace.' "

The issue of Iranian oil brings us to the side of American policy where the Russian Menace began to assume weight as a counterpoise to the British Menace, as we will see also in connection with Poland, although it was not until after Potsdam that the former began to outbalance the latter. So at this point we must turn attention from the western front, the British-American war, to the eastern war, namely, the British-Russian war, which represents the other thread to be disentangled from the Yalta record.

5. The Large Tick

As you read the Yalta papers published by the State Department, you will find no important reference to Greece.

It was nowhere on the Yalta agenda. The record seems to show that at the plenary sessions there were only a couple of passing remarks made about Greece (though you also can't help noticing that these passing remarks are downright mysterious). It would seem that Greece played no role at Yalta.

You could not make a bigger mistake about Yalta. the British-Russian war over Greece loomed big over the conference. Its impact on the conference is a vital element in understanding the deal over Poland. To see why, we have to go back.

To begin with, the British interest in Greece is one of the world's most blatant examples of finance capitalist imperialism. By the end of the Greek War of Independence of 1821, Greece owed British bankers fifteen million dollars, though she had actually borrowed only one-third of that amount! Between 1825 and 1898, Greek governments borrowed four hundred million dollars from London banks (still getting only a fraction of this sum).

By 1945 all loans had been paid off *sevenfold* (interest, carrying charges, etc.) but the entire face sum of the debt was still owed to British banks. Modern Greece (up to 1935 figures, anyway) had been setting aside each year *one-third* of her total income for servicing these loans. Even during the depression of the 1930s the British Shylocks forced Greece to pay in gold, although they themselves were off the gold standard. The money that the Greek government did receive from the loans went largely into maintaining an army and navy which served as a British adjunct. The poverty stricken people of Greece were slaveys and bondsmen of British capital.

During the German occupation in World War II, of course, it was Hitler who took his turn at plundering and starving Greece. The British reinforced their hoops of gold on the Greek government-in-exile. The December 19 before Yalta, Chancellor of the Exchequer Anderson announced in Parliament that the Greeks had gotten one hundred eighty-five million dollars in loans during the war plus another seventy-one million dollars in market loans. Not long before Yalta, the British Foreign Office presented the Greek government with a memorandum calling on it to "safeguard the rights and securities enjoyed by external loans and to protect the general interests of the bondholders" and "maintain unchanged the rights, privileges and conditions of service which have applied to the government loans since 1898."

But the Greek government was not really in shape to safeguard, protect or ensure anything in Greece, least of all itself — against either the "liberating" Russian troops advancing down to the border from the north, or against the internal anti-Nazi resistance movement which was trying to take over control in southern Greece as the German troops withdrew.

If Britain was going to preserve its golden goose in Greece, it would have to do it itself. This, of course, had been one strong factor behind the British desire that the second front should have been opened up through the Balkan "underbelly."

In October 1944 (this is four months before Yalta) Churchill flew to Moscow to settle the matter. This is the Moscow conference which we have already had occasion to mention in other connections. Churchill's main concern, however, was Greece. He landed October 9; met Stalin in conference the same evening; and spread out his wares without beating about the bush.

Here is Churchill's own unforgettable account — one of the world's great classics:

> The moment was apt for business, so I said, "Let us settle about our affairs in the Balkans. Your armies are in Roumania and Bulgaria. We have interests, missions and agents there. Don't let us get at cross purposes in small ways. So far as Britain and Russia are concerned, how would it do for you to have 90 per cent predominance in Roumania, for us to have 90 per cent of the say in Greece, and go 50-50 about Yugoslavia?" While this was being translated I wrote out on a half-sheet of paper:

Country	Russia	Great Britain	The Others
Roumania	90%		10%
Greece	10%	90% (In accord with USA)	
Yugoslavia	50%	50%	
Hungary	50%	50%	
Bulgaria	75%		25%

> I pushed this across to Stalin, who had by then heard the translation. There was a slight pause. Then he took his blue pencil and made a large tick upon it, and passed it back to us. It was all settled in no more time than it takes to set down. . . .

> After this there was a long silence. The pencilled paper lay in the center of the table. At length I said, "Might it not be thought rather cynical if it seemed we had disposed of these issues, so fateful to millions of

people in such an offhand manner? Let us burn the paper." "No, you keep it," said Stalin. (P. 198.)

Two days later, still at Moscow, Churchill included the percentage figures on paper along with a note to Stalin.

As I said, they would be considered crude, and even callous, if they were exposed to the scrutiny of the Foreign Offices and diplomats all over the world. Therefore they could not be the basis of the of any public document, certainly not at the present time. . . . (P. 202.)

In a week British troops were landing in Southern Greece to take over. Thus began the British invasion of the country.

Along with British howitzers came the quislings, King George (the same British hireling who, before the war, had replaced a democratically elected Greek government with the fascist dictator Metaxas) and Premier Papandreou, the puppet leader of the "Liberal Party."

A genuine national revolutionary upsurge of the Greek people answered in massive protest, if anything held beck by the leadership of the Stalinist heads of the EAM (liberation movement) and ELAS (its military arm). For a whole period the Stalinist leadership walked a tightrope between restraining or moderating anti-British action on the one hand and retaining its leadership of the angry masses on the other.

On November 7, Churchill sent a memo to Eden: "In my opinion, having paid the price we have to Russia for freedom of action in Greece, we should not hesitate to use British troops to support . . . Papandreou." (*Churchill*, vol. 6, P. 250.) He hoped troops would "not hesitate to shoot when necessary."

Open civil war began December 3; the police executed a cold-blooded machinegun massacre of an unarmed demonstration of men, women and children. The correspondent for the N.Y. *Post* and Overseas News Agency cabled home: "without provocation." In his book Churchill takes responsibility for the orders to shoot: "It is no use doing these things by halves."

He wired the British general: "Do not, however, hesitate to act as if you were in a conquered city where a local rebellion is in progress." He explains proudly that he "had in mind Arthur Balfour's celebrated telegram in the 80s to the British authorities in Ireland: `don't hesitate to shoot.'"

The whole world cried out in outrage against this open, crude, brutal rape of a nation, which is not surpassed by any of Britain's previous crimes or by any of Stalin's before or since. Churchill himself writes that "the vast majority of the American press violently condemned our action." In England even the London *Times* as well as the Manchester *Guardian* pronounced their censures. In Parliament the attack was led by Acland, Bevan, Shinwell (the Atlee Laborite coalitionists stood with the assassins like a rock.) But —

> Stalin, however, adhered strictly and faithfully to our agreement of October, and during all the long weeks of fighting the Communists in the streets of Athens not one word of reproach came from *Pravda* or *Izvestia.*

We have already seen that in this climate of shocked world opinion, Stettinius made a statement to dissociate the U.S. from the heinous crime, at least by implication; even though at the very same time the U.S. command in Italy was helping the British invasion of Greece by sending planes. We have also seen that Churchill was outraged by American hypocrisy, *Sherwood* says that about this time "he felt that another Big Three conference must be held without a moment's delay."

But in the last analysis it was Stalin who saved Britain's bacon.

Churchill was absolutely convinced (and every historian must agree) that Moscow faithfully executed its deal and did everything possible to quench the revolutionary fire in Greece *short of* losing leadership of the mass movement. Being no idiot, Churchill knew why fighting still went on. In January he stated that the British troops were preventing a situation —

> . . . in which all forms of government would have been swept away, and naked, triumphant Trotskyism installed. I think Trotskyism is a better definition of Greek Communism and certain other sects than the normal word. It has the advantage of being equally hated in Russia.

By "Trotskyism" he simply meant revolutionary workers not subservient to Moscow. Trotskyist groups were not in control. Churchill understood that Moscow had to be gingerly in putting on its straitjacket.

He also understood that, if even now the British stake in Greece could be preserved only by the most ruthless terror, even this terror would not serve were the Kremlin to change the CP's signal from "all brakes on" to "open up the throttle."

We have seen the stake that Greece represented for this empire in decline. We have seen the blood that Churchill unhesitatingly let spurt in order to save this stake. We have seen the world-wide contumely that he grimly faced in order to do his imperialist duty.

And therefore we have also seen the biggest single reason why, chafing and dragging feet, Churchill found it impossible at Yalta to dig his heels into the ground and make a stand against the Russian rape of Poland. Even Churchill! Even he who acutely realized the danger of Russian domination of the Continent, unlike the U.S. statesmen who were pursuing their own imperialist business of chopping down Britain while Britain was slicing off Greece.

It is this divided interest of the British watchdog of empire which made it impossible for him to *agree* to the Russian fate for Poland while at the same time he was forced to *tolerate* what he knew was happening and was going to happen.

It was torn minds like this, on the part of the Western side, which at Yalta translated into the *surface* ambiguity of the conference decisions — even though, as we shall prove, neither Churchill nor Roosevelt were naive about what had been decided *de facto*.

On two occasions Stalin had to twist Churchill's arm for a reminder. These are the otherwise mysterious references to Greece actually recorded.

At the 5th plenary session, while the Polish question was still sticking, Stalin suddenly inquired from Churchill what was happening in Greece. In reply Churchill mentioned the British trade-union delegation to Greece [safe social-imperialists], said he had not seen their report but understood "that they had had rather a rough time in Greece and they were very much obliged to Marshal Stalin for not having taken too great an interest in Greek affairs. I thank the Marshal for his help."

"I only wanted to know for information. We have no intention of intervening there in any way," said Stalin.

At the 6th plenum, Molotov made an amendment to a conference document on liberated Europe to the effect that the Big Three would support those elements which had fought against the Nazis. The other Two opposed it, naturally, understanding that it could only be a legal cover for giving the Stalinist quislings in East Europe official sanction. Molotov later withdrew the amendment without fuss since it had been made in the first place only to bare teeth in a warning snarl. In the discussion on this amendment, Matthews' minutes capture a priceless vignette, a seemingly irrelevant interlude, which we reproduce textually:

> *STALIN (to Churchill who was about to say something)*: "Are you worried about Greece?" *(laughing)*.

Churchill denied that he was feeling anxious. Bohlen's minutes add: "Marshal Stalin said he thought it would have been very dangerous if he had allowed other forces than his own to go into Greece." (He may have been referring to Tito's troops.)

And so the mute deal was consummated: a Greece for a Poland. There were two sequels:

(1) On the day that the Yalta agreement was announced, it was also announced to the world that the ELAS Stalinist leaders had accepted a pact with the Greek government to disarm its fighters.

(2) Reporting to Parliament in defense of the Yalta sellout of Poland, Churchill made the connection as openly as one has a right to expect:

> I felt bound to proclaim my confidence in Soviet good faith in the hope of procuring it. In this I was encouraged by Stalin's behavior about Greece.

6. Peace and Quiet

Coming now directly to the Polish phase of the Yalta agenda, we have in effect already explained the political motivations behind the sellout. But of course, it may be objected that no sellout has yet been shown. In fact, do not the liberals and other Democrats insist on the story that Roosevelt left Yalta convinced that Poland had been saved from the bear's clutches, that the only trouble was that Russia later violated the agreement, and that no one could have known better at the time, and that the outcries are being made today on the basis of "20-20 hindsight"? Who could have known, they ask? Should

Roosevelt have irresponsibly broken the precious Big Three unity simply out of suspicion?

It can be proved up to the hilt that when Roosevelt and Churchill left Yalta, they knew that Poland was a goner. There is room here only to summarize the evidence. The point involved is not simply to impugn the sincerity of their protestations, for we have already seen more than enough reason not to worry about the public sincerity or morality of these gentlemen, but to exhibit the political meaning of the Yalta deal, which is only obscured by the liberal myth.

To be sure, it is not decisive merely to point out that Roosevelt had no right to have any illusions about Russia's intentions for Poland. He was dealing with the brigands who had *already* joined in the ravishment of Poland in alliance with Hitler! If that is considered water under the bridge, then we must point out that by the time of Yalta the Stalinist totalitarian terror in Poland was in full swing and known to the whole world. If we were merely to list the already known acts of forceful suppression and purging of all opponents, including even (already!) the purging of the first *Stalinists,* there are few people who would seriously consider the theory that adult statesmen could keep blinding themselves to the obvious. The month before Yalta, the Moscow embassy (Harriman) had sent in an adequate report on the Polish terror.

Was Roosevelt really naive about this? In a Roosevelt memo to Stettinius dated September 29, 1944, we read the following realistic statement of his attitude:

> In regard to the Soviet government, it is true that we have no idea as yet what they have in mind, but we have to remember that in their occupied territory they will do more or less what they wish. We cannot afford to get into a position of merely recording protests on our part unless there is a chance of some of the protests being heeded.

This is a statement of Roosevelt's strategy of not fighting Russian demands on Eastern Europe, in the name of that hallowed Big Three unity which was necessary to organize the world. Should the Polish people be so narrow minded and parochial as to get in the way of this glorious objective?

Surely Stalin left him with little reason to misunderstand at Yalta. At the 3rd plenum, Stalin made his long speech on the subject, including:

Now as a military man I must say what I demand of a country liberated by the Red Army. First, there should be peace and quiet in the wake of the army. . . . When I compare the agents of both governments I find the Lublin ones are useful and the others the contrary. The military must have peace and quiet. The military will support such a government and I cannot do otherwise. Such is the situation.

How much more brutal did Stalin have to get before he could be sure that Roosevelt understood?

Moreover, in advance of Yalta the State Department had already conceded the following in black on white in its own Briefing Book: that the U.S. "probably would not oppose predominant Soviet influence in the area" but wished that American influence not be "completely nullified." The latter phrase was spelled out to include "some degree" of commercial and financial access to the Polish economy.

After Yalta, *Leahy* writes,

Personally I did not believe that the dominating Soviet influence could be excluded from Poland, but I did not think it was possible to give to a reorganized Polish government an external appearance of independence. (P. 352.)

Isn't that frank?

Leahy testifies that he told Roosevelt at Yalta, "Mr. President this [agreement on Poland] is so elastic that the Russians can stretch it all the way from Yalta to Washington without ever technically breaking it." Roosevelt replied: "I know, Bill — I know it. But it's the best I can do for Poland at this time." (P. 315-6.) Leahy may be charged with predating hindsight, but he cannot be charged with trying to smear Roosevelt by misquotation.

After the agreement was made, the Yalta record has Churchill saying painfully:

CHURCHILL: Wants to say dec[laration] re Pol[and] will be very heavily attacked in Eng[land]. It will be said we have yielded completely on the frontiers and the whole matter to R[ussia]. . . . However, I will defend it to the best of my ability.

It does not sound like a man who believes he has saved Poland. He sounds like the beaten man he was. No different impression emerges from Churchill's report to Parliament where he tried to defend it "to the best of my ability." I refuse to discuss Russian good faith, he said. It is a mistake to look too far ahead, he said! What is democracy after all, he asked! . . . He does not sound like a naive man.

It is possible to document the charge that Churchill and Roosevelt never even *tried* to fight for the proposals which they themselves thought were vital to assure Poland's independence.

At the October Moscow conference, Churchill had laid down a *sine qua non*:

After the Kremlin dinner we put it bluntly to Stalin that unless Mikolajczyk had 50-50 plus himself, the Western World would not be convinced that the transaction was bona fide and would not believe that an independent Polish government had been set up. (To Roosevelt, *Churchill,* vol. 6, P. 210.)

This proposal *sine qua non* was never even breathed at Yalta.

The State Department's pre-Yalta Briefing Book said that in order to achieve free elections in Poland, "we should sponsor United Nations arrangements for their supervision." This proposal was never even breathed at Yalta.

At Yalta itself, after the 1st plenum, Churchill wired Atlee: "If it can be so arranged that 8 or 10 of these [non-Stalinist Poles] are included in the Lublin government it would be to our advantage to recognize this government at once." (*Churchill,* vol. 6, P. 328.) But the record shows that neither he nor Roosevelt ever proposed adding that number of non-Stalinists!

The record does show that the U.S. did put forward a proposal to replace the Polish president with a "presidential committee" of three. The record also shows that it never fought for this proposal, which the Russians rejected immediately, and quickly abandoned it.

After Yalta, the State Department soothed Polish Ambassador Ciechanowski with the claim that the U.S. would insist on a new Polish government that was "equally balanced." (*Ciechanowski,* P.361.) This was a falsehood; it had never been mentioned at Yalta.

Stettinius' book on Yalta is a straight apologia, but he admits:

> As a result of this military situation, it was not a question of what Great Britain and the U.S. would permit Russia to do in Poland, but what the two countries could persuade the Soviet Union to accept. (P. 301.)

We have seen what they did not even try to persuade the Russians to accept.

What then was the bargaining at Yalta about? It is as plain as an oversize pikestaff that the Two were holding out for the best possible *window dressing* for what they knew was a foregone conclusion.

It took the form mainly of a prolonged higgle-haggle over the *wording* of the agreement on the Polish government which all were to recognize. It boiled down to this: the Russians held for wording which meant a mere *reorganization based on* the present Lublin government, with non-Stalinists added, while Britain held out for wording which would imply that a brand new government was being set up; and Roosevelt mainly reminded them both that only terminology was involved and they ought to get together. That is all, absolutely all, that the main disagreement amounted to. The final text used some language ("new situation," "new government") that the British might be able to use, while it clearly defined the government in the Russian terms (the Lublin government *"reorganized* on a broader democratic basis . . ."). Churchill won another hunk of window dressing when Stalin finally agreed that Mikolajczyk would be defined as a "nonfascist" and permitted to participate in the government!

The strange thing is that the Yalta record quotes Churchill himself as referring to the window dressing character of the dispute: "He said this might be an ornament, but nevertheless an important ornament."

And here, of course, we also have the significance of Roosevelt's repeated appeals to Stalin to keep in mind the Polish-American vote. (At the 3rd plenum, Roosevelt used this apropos of his request to Stalin to make a deviation from the Curzon line: "There are six or seven million Poles in the U.S. . . . Most Poles, like the Chinese, want to save face. . . . It would make it easier for me at home if the Soviet government would give something to Poland.")

It was at the 6th plenum that Roosevelt made his appeal for a "gesture" on the government composition question to appease the Poles back home:

> He said he felt it was very important for him in the U.S. that there be some gesture made for the six million Poles there, indicating that the U.S. was in some way involved with the question of freedom of elections. . . . He repeated that he felt, however, that it was only matter of words and details. . . .

No, the facts leave no doubt as to the nature of the Yalta bargaining on the Polish question. Sellout is a dirty word, to be sure. Anyone has a right to argue that Roosevelt and Churchill were justified in selling out — pardon, *neglecting Poland's rights* in order to achieve more important ends labelled "Big Three unity," like Big Three unity on the rape of Greece, like Big Three unity on dividing Rumania 90-10, like Big Three unity on the suppression of small nations and colonies. But no one has the right any longer to take seriously the myth that Roosevelt and Churchill were country boys who bought a Polish goldbrick from the Moscow city slicker.

7. Strange Banners

> They played excellent music and carried strange-looking banners, the meaning of which was not apparent to me.

Thus Leahy described the Russian band that met the Roosevelt party when they landed for the Yalta conference. You can take this as the symbol for Yalta.

We wrote above that Roosevelt and Churchill were not deceived about the meaning of the Polish deal. But no one can defend Roosevelt from the charge of being taken for a ride if, paradoxically, the charge is only made broad enough. He was not taken in on Poland, but he was taken in on the struggle for the world.

One of the eeriest scenes in the Yalta record is not from the recent publication but from Churchill, who records a toast made by Stalin on the evening of February 8, when many a toast was drunk, although Byrnes suspected Vishinsky of watering his vodka.

It is hard to say whether Stalin was getting a bit maudlin or whether it was just his usual style. (Churchill remarks: "I had never suspected that he could be so expansive.") Stalin began:

> I am talking as an old man; that is why I am talking so much. But I want to drink to our alliance. [How wonderfully intimate it is!] . . . I know that some circles will regard this remark as naive. In an alliance the allies should not deceive each other. Perhaps that is naive? Experienced diplomatists may say, "Why should I not deceive my ally?" But I as a naive man think it best not to deceive my ally, even if he is a fool. . . .

"Even if he is a fool . . ."! Anyone acquainted with Stalin's mode of thought and style cannot avoid feeling that at this strange moment, standing knowingly on the verge of power such as few conquerors have wielded over the world, the old butcher could no longer contain the chortling contempt for his allies that slipped out.

He was not unjustified. It is true that he happily faced a whole stratum of American policy makers (bipartisan in makeup) who were so intent on inheriting the British Empire that they could not see what was happening in the world. It is true that the Americans undoubtedly told themselves that Russia, bled white by Germany, would be near-prostrate after the war and could not offer a serious menace to the U.S. For they viewed Russia solely as just another imperialist power, like any other, understanding no more than America's rulers do today that Stalinism's weapons against the old capitalist societies are not primarily military, the military being auxiliary to the political dynamism of its anticapitalist appeal.

And if Roosevelt and the U.S. delegation were really exultant after Yalta, as *Sherwood* states, it was because they were wallowing in the conception that they had succeeded in forging a "Big Three unity" that could organize the whole world under its suzerainty, *while the United States colossus of wealth and power would be the arbiter of the Three, precisely the role which Roosevelt systematically and deliberately sought to play at Yalta.* To shoot at this status of Chairman of the

Board of Earth, Inc., the U.S. could not do without "Big Three unity." And so they had to believe that it was also possible; that is, that it was possible to achieve a "normal" imperialist relationship with the imperialist rival Russia as with imperialist rival Britain, within the "normal" framework of power politics, registering the existing relationship of forces.

A "normal" imperialist relation with Stalinist Russia? We have a term for it today. It means exactly the same as the famous "peaceful coexistence." The GOP dinosaurs — who are against "peaceful coexistence" on reactionary grounds, i.e., because they want a more warlike policy against Russia — are well advised from their standpoint to make Yalta their cussword.

But there was no pro-Stalinism or treason at Yalta. The basic fact is that always, in whatever form, the bourgeois statesmen know only the choice between attempting an imperialist peace with rivals (Yalta) or drifting or driving toward imperialist war with rivals (Truman-Eisenhower).

And in either case the American would-be rulers of the declining capitalist world have shown the political stigmata of declining ruling classes: disorientation and blindness, which often look like stupidity and ignorance.

Before Yalta, this meant that they had not the slightest understanding of what Stalinism is, and they still haven't, although they have painfully learned by the contusions on their rear that it is at any rate an irreconcilable enemy of capitalism.

In the Second World War climate of American power politics, there was a whole generation of liberals and others who were sitting ducks for the Stalinists' planned campaign to convince the Americans that they were on their way back to capitalism like respectable folk. According to *Ciechanowski* (P. 249), Stalin utilized the Tehran conference to fill up Roosevelt with such a load of this suckerbait that the latter exuded it from his pores. And everyone knows Roosevelt's reference at Yalta to the Chinese Stalinists as "the so-called Communists." Just before Yalta, Molotov had (confidentially!) disclosed to Hurley that "Russians are not supporting Chinese Communists who are not Communists at all"; Hurley had rushed to send this revelation to Washington, whence Roosevelt had already left. Washington hurled the sensation via the ether to Roosevelt at Yalta, who got the glad tidings on February 5.

All this required no "conspiracy" in the McCarthy-Knowland sense; the political soil was thirsty for it. American imperialism, with its world strategy, *needed* a rationale, a theory, that made room for its version of "Big Three unity." And if the actual elaboration of this theory was a friendly collaboration of good patriots and good Stalinoids, the details of its creation are of secondary interest.

Today the right wing of American imperialism is pushing toward another war, this time (they think) *really* to settle the matter of world domination. And the liberals, who today have no more idea than they ever had of how to counterpose a democratic foreign policy to the Truman-Eisenhower policy of imperialism, cannot understand the nature of this imperialism they support even when it is practically spelled out for them by the men who divided up the world at Yalta.

It is a psychological as well as a political fact: *only those who are ready to struggle against them are ready to understand,* down to the bottom, the nature of the rival imperialist camps that are battling for the right to exploit the world, capitalist and Stalinist imperialism.

Labor Action
April 4, 1955

America as Arbiter
An Essay in Historical Perspective

Introductory Note

No event in postwar history showed the overlord pattern more clearly than the intervention of the United States government to hold back the dogs of war in the invasion of Egypt to grab the Suez Canal. The dogs in this case were the allied forces of England, France and Israel. President Eisenhower got out his bullwhip, held up his hand like a traffic cop, and whipped the dogs back to their kennels. The Overlord was doing his job: in American eyes, the Western coalition lived only to defeat America's *enemy, and here these three dogs were trying to grab off something for themselves. . . . The Russians were deeply disappointed, for a Western rape of the Suez Canal would have given the Middle East over to the Kremlin's sphere of influence. As it was they had to be content with the diversion it provided while they invaded Hungary to crush the revolution against their rule.*

The Suez crisis forced the United States to assert its overlordship publicly and explicitly: this was what was most distinctive about it.

The essay that follows was first given as a lecture, before it was written up and published in the October 1, 1956 issue of Labor Action. *I think it was one of those cases where it was a question of articulating and concretizing what many other people were beginning to see.*

H. D.

The role of the U.S. in the Suez canal affair has been more complex than is indicated by the true statement that Washington has been backing London and Paris in their colonialist attempt to beat Egypt into line.

If anyone thinks that a good leftist policy can be manufactured automatically simply by inverting whatever the Right says, here is an opportunity to hail John Foster Dulles as a savior of peace or what-have-you. That would be quite as fantastic as the current hints from France's ultra-chauvinists that Dulles is a heinous enemy of Western civilization and all that it holds dear.

It would be perhaps sufficient to explain, as we have explained before, that the interests of American imperialism in the Suez crisis are by no means identical with those of London-Paris (and the interests of London and Paris are not even identical with each other) even though all these powers have common and overweening interests as bastions of world capitalism and as the kingpins of the NATO alliance.

That is true; and it is a good thing to keep in mind when the dilemma of the colonialist powers becomes so difficult that the latent differences between the allies, beginning as cracks, are pried apart into open splits. So weighty has been the force of world public opinion against the crude assault on Egypt that the colonialists have had a minimum of room in which to maneuver.

But it is not *only* a matter of differences in interest as between U.S. imperialism and its fellow imperialists in Europe. To put it this way is to view the U.S. solely as one imperialism among others. That is not enough. The United States is more than that.

It is the mediator and arbiter of its imperialist camp. There has never been anything better than the course of the Suez crisis to put flesh and substance on this abstract idea to which we have often pointed. At the same time it is also the key to an understanding of the twists in U.S. policy — which Nasser claims is a "puzzle" to him, and which French and British journalists are now engaged in lambasting.

The United States is certainly not on the side of Egypt in this conflict; nor has it been *simply* a supporter of Britain and France; and no one at all ever took seriously some tentative attempts by Dulles to pose as a neutral referee as between the colonialist powers and the small country; nor can the U.S. course be entirely explained merely as a reflex of particularist U.S. interests.

These are four things it is *not.* What is left is an aspect of contemporary American imperialism which is relatively new and unexplored. It is indicated when publicists speak of the U.S. as the "leader of the free world," which is their code language for saying the same thing that we are saying here.

Make this contrast:

Back in the period of the First World War, the internal relationship in (say) the Entente camp, as between the major member-imperialisms in that camp, was roughly that of *equals.* No single belligerent dominated the alliance; that, incidentally, was one reason why no really unified military command was possible, either.

At the other end of the spectrum of possibilities, look at the internal relationship of the Stalinist war camp at least under Stalin: namely, the relationship between the Russian *master* and the East European *puppets* or slave-states.

But these two cases do not exhaust the types of relationship inside an imperialist camp. Since the Second World War, the relationship that has grown up in the atlantic bloc has been neither one of approximate equality nor of master-slave. It has been, rather, that of *overlord and vassal* (to continue the figure of speech). The United States has increasingly tended to assume the role of overlord in the Western capitalists camp, as the only one of the capitalist powers which still has the military and economic, industrial and financial power to bear the burden of arming, nourishing, rewarding, reconstructing, bribing and replenishing other states. An "overlord," one must remember, had other and powerful lords below him, not only serfs. The king began not as an autocrat but a "first among equals."

This position of eminence has been granted the U.S. by reluctant allies not simply out of gratitude or in payment for Marshall Plan aid, nor was it imposed upon them by force, but because the entire capitalist world faces a common enemy in the face of which its internal squabbles could be disastrous, and may yet be; this common enemy is Russia and its fellow Stalinist allies and/or satellites.

The Russian empire is not simply another imperialist rival. It is a rival exploitative *social system*, which is as anticapitalist as it is antisocialist. From the vantage point of the bourgeoisie, the antisocialism of the Stalinists is a very fine point of secondary interest if any; the victory of this rival system means the death of capitalism, of this bourgeoisie's system, and that is what quite understandably concerns *them.*

The consequence of this fact is that we do not today have the same thing as the balance-of-power politics of World War I (or even II) days. In the classic pattern that led up to 1914, the rival imperialist powers "chose up sides" like kids on a sandlot; Italy, for instance, changed sides with the aplomb of a baseball player being traded from the Dodgers to the Yankees.

Today the capitalist powers do not have this kind of latitude in choosing their side, or in declining to choose any side, and this must be said with emphasis in spite of the strength of so-called "neutralism" in Europe. The division of the world between the two war camps is not primarily the outcome of balance-of-power jockeying, but is primarily a reflection of the given world division between the rival *social systems* of capitalism and Stalinism.

The looming world war is not a struggle simply of one set of imperialist powers against another set. It will be a war for the survival of *capitalism* or its rival. In the First World War, each participant could feel that it was only partially committed to its own side; it need not have felt that *everything* it had was riding on its colors. (Hence, for example, the phenomenon of the respect shown by the contending armies in going easy on bombing and destroying each others basic industrial targets — phenomenon that was already on the way out in World War II.) In the war of systems which looms, there will be no holds barred.

It is under these new conditions that the necessity arises of subordinating the conflicting interests and pulls within the capitalist camp to an arbiter, lest the camp be pulled apart.

At the same time, that supra-national imperialist arbiter is also one of the contending imperialisms, itself, and not just a disinterested umpire. This immediately introduces a complicating element of conflict within the very institution of this arbiter, but it is not the only one, and it cannot be avoided.

The United States has naturally become that overlord — that arbiter — and its status *works* as long as (and to the extent that) the lesser "lords" feel the pressure of the Russian threat. American domination over Europe feeds on Stalinism's very existence. American imperialism could never have attained its present position of preeminence except by the grace of the Kremlin.

But while the institution of the arbiter can mediate interimperialist squabbles, it cannot hope to abolish them.

This is the fascinating problem of the interrelationships between the imperialist powers which has been illuminated by the shifting course of the Suez dispute.

It has been especially illuminating in the Suez case because here was an international crisis in which Russia was *not* directly involved. Where Stalinist power is directly involved, of course, it has been easier for the U.S. to "take the lead of the free world," i.e. (to translate) to marshal its junior allies behind it — though even here it has had squabbles with the latter, as with France over Indochinese policy.

The case of Suez introduces a greater complexity; for from the viewpoint of an *individual* imperialist state, how much difference does it make if it is stripped of sources of exploitation by the Stalinist foe or if it is so despoiled by the exploited peoples themselves? In the name of Unity Against the Russian Menace, it is a little difficult for any given colonialist power to resign itself gracefully to losing *now* that which the aforesaid Russian menace may try to take away later.

Of course, when Nasser nationalized the Suez Canal, this was not yet equivalent to England and France's definitive loss of all the perquisites of colonialism, and so the preceding paragraph is an exaggeration; but it is an exaggeration that points accurately to the drive that pushes Mollet and Eden into their present posture of bitter intransigence.

On the international scale, capitalism faces a problem which is analogous to one which it faces within each national capitalist system, but which it *cannot* solve in the same way.

Here is the problem as it has always existed historically *within* a national capitalist system: If each individual capitalist unremittingly and always pursued only his individual profit interest without regard to any other consideration, in proverbial dog-eat-dog fashion, then capitalism itself would tear itself apart in short order. The internecine conflict which is inherent in the structure of capitalist competition must be mediated, at least enough to keep the warring particles from flying apart, at least enough so as to moderate the self-destructive tendencies from shattering the framework of the system itself.

This is done in part by agreements "in restraint of trade" (as the antitrust laws naively put it), that is, in restraint of the inherent tendencies of really "free" enterprise. Even very short-sighted businessmen, who keep their eyes tightly glued on the elusive fast buck just before their nose and not an inch beyond, can usually see the advantages of curbing their impulses to knife the competitor if the immediate result (say, a price war) would be mutually suicidal.

But as the system grows more complicated, and the self-destructive tendencies of capitalism grow in areas further and further removed from the immediate economic plane, it is only the more farsighted leaders of the system who can continue to see clearly what sacrifices have to be made by capitalists-as-individual-profitmakers in order to ensure their continued existence as capitalists, i.e., to ensure the continued health of the system.

Here are some examples from yesterday:

● Should the pillars of the business community oppose the newfangled notions of universal free education for the common herd, which will cost hard money in more taxes, or should they accede to this demand, at least under pressure, since an educated working class will be more productive in the long run under modern industrial conditions?

● Is it more profitable to keep your immediate wage bill down by paying starvation wages, or is it more profitable in the long run to pay $5 a week more and set up an assembly line system (Fordism)?

More difficult kinds of sacrifice (sacrifice of the immediate buck) were demanded of capitalists by the New Deal, whose braintrusters more or less consciously set themselves the problem just as we are presenting it here. This is what was behind capitalists' resentment of "that man in the White House".

These were more difficult only because they were harder to see by a capitalist class which (like its working class) was still so politically backward. The reforms of the New Deal were, in essence, old stuff in Europe. Today the whole capitalist class has become used to them, and even Adlai Stevenson proclaims that the "conquests" of the New Deal have been irreversibly accepted by the Republicans themselves.

Now the ability of individuals to see, and respond to, the longer-range interests of their class, as against keeping myopic eyes fastened to the chalkline of immediate profit, is not simply a personal factor or a function of IQ.

For one thing, those capitalist leaders who live in the upper reaches of the financial world, with the most far-flung and varied interests, have naturally the widest horizons; they can get the best bird's eye view of the needs of the system as a whole, as against (to go to the opposite) the small sweat shopper types. This consideration is germane to such a question as the "internationalism" (interventionism) of Eastern finance-capitalist Republicanism, as distinct from the political cultural laggers who give some of its tone to Midwestern tendencies in the GOP, from Taftism to McCarthy-type McCarthyism.

But even these wider-scanners cannot see the whole house within which they live as long as their own perspective remains bound within it. Hence it has often been true historically, and for good reason, that vital reforms for the fundamental health of capitalism have been put through not under the leadership of *individuals* who are themselves practicing capitalists, but rather under the leadership of individuals who themselves (in training, tradition, perspective) stand outside the system, or removed from its centers, though allied with it in all interests.

The classic examples of this have been Bismarck, the Prussian Junker who was able to carry through the national unification of Germany where the pettifogging German bourgeoisie was too nerveless to fulfill its own class destiny; and F. D. Roosevelt, the "Country Gentleman in the White House" from the Hudson patroon family, who had no shortsighted and obsolete class prejudices hanging over from the past to prevent him from accepting methods which at first pained a good portion of the capitalist class and its experienced flunkies.

The prime instrument which serves to mediate and arbitrate the otherwise racking internal conflicts of the capitalist class is — its state.

Now we have reviewed the internal-national capitalist problem not because its answers can be transferred point by point to the international scene, but only because its *problems* can be so transferred — if not point by point then at any rate in outline.

We may remark in passing that these problems are thus shown to be unanswerable without the analogous solution of setting up a *world-state*, superseding the present capitalist national sovereignties, such as World Federalists and other bourgeois utopians dream of so futilely; but it is the existence of the analogous *problems* themselves which provides the steam behind the contemporary rash of talk about world government and which gives a color of life to bourgeois schemes for supranational federalism, "Council of Europe," etc.

The capitalist world might well have become overwhelmingly self-conscious about these systemic problems without the rise of such a world-scale social rival to its own system as is constituted by the anticapitalist (bureaucratic collectivist) power of Russia — perhaps, in due time; that is, with the increase in its own decline.

Tarzan could become conscious that he was a man only after meeting other human beings; world capitalism as such, if we can make such an abstraction for the purpose of an analogy, could become conscious of itself as a social system with its own needs only after running into another social system.

To some extent this already happened in the course of the First European Revolution of 1917 — 1923, when the specter of socialist revolution raised its head on a continental scale; but the U.S. was not really involved; and anyway that prospect was put down in a few years.

As we said, perhaps world capitalism's consciousness of the above-discussed type of *problems* would have matured without the catalyst constituted by the rise of a bureaucratic collectivist world power counterposed to capitalism as such. After all, in the past too, supranational centralization has been a characteristic accompaniment of the precipitous *decline* of a social system, even where that social system was not being threatened by a rival society but merely dying in its boots.

Thus it was that the acme of the ancient slave society, the Roman Empire, in its centuries of disintegration twisted in the throes of bureaucratic centralization and in forms of statification which one might almost call totalitarian without being too anachronistic.

Thus also it was in the period of the *decline* of feudalism that the local particularities and petty sovereignties of the lords were overcome to make way for absolute monarchy, which already reflected the impact of the rival social system that was destroying it.

But such analogies from the past can only be suggestive, since today *one* of the most powerful driving forces behind the impulse to international consolidation is new and modern: the existence for the first time, in a real sense, of a world economy (we are referring to the world *capitalist* economy, in the capitalist world) — the interdependent world character of the economy and the productive forces. The achievement of this stage is one of the conquests of capitalism of which it can be proud — and which is therefore racking it with unresolvable problems.

Who has the most farsighted view of the nature of this capitalist problem, among the capitalist statesmen and thinkers? Who has the widest bird's-eye view? There are several contenders for this status, each of whom share a piece, though they tend to think that the sector which they can see is the whole vista of foreign policy.

Thinking of the internal-national problem, we can perhaps ask analogously who it is that, in a sense, stands outside or removed from the world-capitalist centers (by tradition, training, perspective — as before) and, though bourgeois in sympathy, can hope to see a wider sector of the house out of which he is leaning. . . .

The question points to such figures as Nehru, brought up ambivalently in conflict with capitalist imperialism, even in hatred of it, yet tied to bourgeois values and conscious of his responsibilities to his own native capitalism.

This is the source of those truths about the Western war camp which Nehru has been capable of pointing out; the source of those warnings against suicidal measures by the capitalist camp which lies in the "neutralism" of his type. (The sharp limitations of neutralism are a topic that has been discussed often and at length, and would be a digression here.)

The same semidetachment from, yet basic involvement in, the capitalist world can be noted, in a quite different form, with regard to the social democracy in many countries. Here indeed we have a bridge between the internal-national problems and the analogous world problems of capitalism.

Internally, the social democracy has often functioned as that necessary "alien" class force which alone was able to put through needed bourgeois reforms when the bourgeoisie itself was unable to rise to the task, or indeed, not infrequently, to mobilize counterrevolutionary forces to put down socialist aspirations when the bourgeoisie itself was paralyzed with panic.

On the scale of world problems, the social democracy in governmental control of quite a few countries has stressed hospitality to attempts at world-cooperation (UN-ism, chitchat about united Europe, etc.), to mention its formally "progressive" side; and also has not blanched from the task of doing for its bourgeoisie's imperialism what no bourgeois party could effectively get away with — which is the present role of Mollet's Socialist Party as the current vanguard of colonialist oppression in North africa. Yet this same Mollet, who with "socialist" speeches on his lips sends French youth to get killed murdering Algerian patriots, could recently, in a much publicized interview, tell Washington some home truths about the shortsightedness of its cold war policies vis-à-vis Russia.

It is (to coin a phrase) no accident that last week it was a gathering in Europe quaintly calling itself the "Liberal International" — a talkfest of so-called liberal parties from European countries — who raised the slogan of European unity *precisely as a means of jointly organizing European imperialism* against the threat from the colonial and smaller countries to weaken its domination. This was immediately in connection with the Suez crisis.

It is another manifestation of the *problem* which, however futilely, stimulates hopes of supranational leadership as a defense mechanism of imperialism.

There are other candidates for post of he-who-sees-furthest among capitalism's world problems, i.e., whose position is such that they see a wider sector.

From the point of view of simple experience as manipulators of world forces, Britain, on the background of its centuries of responsibility for administering an empire, is analogous to (say) the board chairman of GM if we think of the United States (with its parochial past) as analogous to a *nouveau riche* who has come into wealth and power by developing local bonanza oil wells but who is just discovering the world outside Texas.

But none of these can aspire to the position which they know is necessary for the safety and self-defense of world capitalism in these days of its decline — that of over all supranational leadership, that of the Arbiter.

That position can only go to the United States by virtue of its overshadowing power, and in spite of its lack of many other qualifications.

Yet what other major power is so raw and *gauche* in world diplomacy, that is, so inexperienced and unskilled in the arts of manipulating and utilizing international forces on a world scale? The United States has never yet had a president who had half the understanding in world politics of a second- string man in the British Foreign Office.

Franklin Roosevelt, for instance? What stands out from a perusal of the notorious Yalta record is not at all any "treason" or "pro-Communism" but rather the overwhelming, sometimes hair-raising but always utter and complete inability of Roosevelt to understand the first thing about Russian Stalinism; and that goes, perforce, for his international rep. Harry Hopkins as well. And Roosevelt was a cultivated, sophisticated and worldly-wise man, compared with the courthouse politician who succeeded him or the brassbound gladhander who followed in due course.

No other nation has ever been pushed into the position of responsibility for a world system such as the American arbiter has had to assume, simply because there has never been room for an arbiter before; and yet there are few major powers that have ever been so haplessly prepared for any kind of world view.

Unprecedented task — perhaps unprecedented incompetence: together, an unprecedented gulf between need and reality.

In a burst of charity we might, at this point, fittingly make a plea for a charitable attitude toward what seems to so many people to be the fantastic ineptness and stupidity of J. F. Dulles. Far be it from us to cast doubt upon this single pillar of consensus in a world of otherwise conflicting opinions. But this theory of stupidity, which has its place, can hardly account for what is now one of the biggest fiascos in Atlantic Alliance strategy, the Suez affair; nor can it account for the far from brilliant record of U.S. foreign policy — one which the Republicans are still living off factionally — under a man who is personally not at all stupid, Dean Acheson.

The truth is that the contemporary role of U.S. imperialism as the Arbiter of the capitalist imperialist world is one that could hardly be adequately played by artful and seasoned performers; it calls forth tremendous difficulties; it imposes a crushing burden; and if the individual Dulles or the State Department is so far from measuring up to it, it is because of the inextricable contradictions that tie up the Atlantic camp of the capitalist world.

It is this that has been dramatized by the course of the Suez crisis, and it is this that provides the intelligible key to the twists of U.S. policy. Here are some of the conflicting strands in the Suez imbroglio — how is an Arbiter to find his way among them?

(1) As everyone knows, France's first concern in the Suez affair is peculiar to it alone: *Algeria*. Mollet and the French press make no bones about it whatsoever. Paris is not half so much interested in the talk about international operation of the canal as it is in uninterrupted French operation of its Algerian colony.

(2) The U.S., as a friend, can sympathize with France's appetite in this respect; but as Arbiter of a more serious operation than that of milking a single country, how far can it afford to antagonize unnecessarily Middle Eastern countries which can retaliate by flirting with The Enemy, Russia?

(3) Britain is interested in the future of its oil and spheres of influence in the Middle East, and expects the Arbiter to keep it happy, for what more valuable ally does it have?

(4) The Arbiter is very anxious to keep Britons happy, and therefore wants to convince the ex-empire that "we" cannot afford to make an open assault on Egypt, because this would be the biggest boon for Russia among all the uncommitted peoples of the world.

(5) At the same time the British suspect, perhaps not without justice, that behind Dulles' very statesmanlike arguments is the economic reality that *American* oil men do not have the same stakes to lose in the Middle East; that, in fact, the closing of the Suez Canal would only make American oil capital virtually completely dominant in the world. In other words, the Arbiter is, at the same time, *one* of the imperialisms to be mediated — a difficulty.

(6) Israel, which has its own interests in the affair, is another disturbing factor: (a) For the most part, even at the height of his imprecations against Nasser, Eden until very recently refrained from saying a good word for Israel's rights to use the canal, with a foresighted eye on future reconciliation with the

Arab bloc. (b) For the State Department, one consequence of the Israeli factor is consideration of the vote at home.

(7) The Baghdad Pact gets shot full of holes; the moribund Arab League revives. How does this fit in?

(8) Cyprus flares up: the British pull back on offers of concessions; the nationalists threaten reprisals if Cyprus is used as a jump off to Suez. The Cypriot struggle is wound into the Suez question.

(9) A military assault on Egypt would take French troops out of Algeria — which could be expected to redouble its guerrilla operations while its oppressor is embroiled elsewhere.

(10) Likewise, the troops used would be in part NATO troops, which have already been mobilized for the purpose. But this is not simply a British-French affair; the commander of these troops is an American, naturally. And furthermore: if the first battle in which NATO troops shoot angry bullets turns out to be against Egypt, as against Algeria, this is not exactly an inducement to uncommitted peoples to get enthusiastic about building the Atlantic Alliance against The Enemy Russia.

(11) Speaking of The Enemy, the Arbiter has to keep in mind (even if in a chauvinist frenzy the British and French are willing to forget) that it is not smart to scotch Nasser through an "international operation" which gives Russia for the first time an official, formal and legal foothold in the Middle East.

(12) On the other hand, if Nasser wins, the Arbiter (this time in its national-U.S. form) has to remember that Panama will get restless about the canal on *its* sovereign territory; and that is happening now.

Since that gives us an even dozen already, we will only hastily mention such internal-political complications as the Labor opposition in Britain, which makes the home front so much different for Eden than it is for Mollet; the domestic-economic considerations of countries like India and their dependence on Suez-carried foreign trade; the fears of other imperialists besides Britain and France, like the Netherlands, of rambunctious colonials being encouraged to act up; etc.

Like chips in an eddying whirl, all the existent issues of imperialism, and many of the besetting political issues at home, get sucked into the Suez affair.

As the Arbiter, the mediator, of this imperialist world, the U.S. tries to do the job of balancing and reconciling, weighing and organizing innumerable conflicting pulls. Can the Arbiter get on top of all this, and pull it together into a coherent policy for a *social system?*

It is a well-nigh hopeless task.

A good stab at it would take brilliant leaders who had the capacity really to understand the world they were trying to defend. It is doubly difficult for representatives of an egocentric imperialism with their class-limited range of thinking. It is triply difficult for such representatives who are far from brilliant and even less experienced.

This, at any rate, is a sketch of the type of *problem* which confronted the U.S. in the Suez affair, as the Arbiter of its war camp, not simply as one imperialist contender among others.

Labor Action
October 1, 1956

The Case of Guatemala

Introductory Note

As this is written, I have recently seen two PBS television documentaries in which the Authorities (in one case Bill Moyers, in another Bill Kurtiss) related the CIA's illegal counterrevolutionary interventions in Guatemala — to overthrow its democratically elected government by force and violence — with no more hesitation about telling the historical facts than if they were recounting Columbus' voyages. It is over a third of a century since it happened, and the truth can now be told. In contrast, when Guatemalan democracy was crushed by the CIA's secret conspiracy in 1954, the simple truth was hotly denied not only by the Washington liars paid to do that job but also by the leading liberal spokesmen in this country.

Liberal? Why, when Professor Robert J. Alexander, the Socialist Party's leading light in the field of Latin American scholarship, published his next book, he scouted the charge against our CIA as a baseless lie. Yet the basic facts were already fairly well known in the less official circles of American consciousness, even at that time: this was brought out in Labor Action not only in the articles below but also in articles not here reprinted.

H. D.

With the fatality which inheres in U.S. foreign policy, in another place where Stalinist influence has obtained a foothold, Guatemala, Washington is doing its utmost to push the country deeper into the arms of Stalinists.

Here in this "banana republic" dominated economically by the United Fruit Company, American economic imperialism is doing the job of greasing the road for Stalinist influence which, in Indochina, was done by French colonialism.

In the Americas as in Asia, Stalinism feeds on the crimes of imperialism and capitalism; it appeals to the anticapitalist sentiments of the peoples. But this appeal which it is able to use for its own purposes is not merely "propaganda." It is also based on the truth.

In Guatemala the Arbenz regime, led by a social reform party which has also accepted the Stalinist party into the government as a coalition partner, has dared to take steps against United Fruit, the chief foreign exploiter of

Guatemalan labor and Guatemalan resources. A good part of the conflict hinges around this. On the one hand, the Arbenz government has leaned on Stalinist support in mobilizing resistance to the foreign exploiter. On the other hand, the Stalinists have utilized Guatemalan antiimperialism in order to extend their own influence. And the U.S. has been trying to paint Guatemala as "Communist-dominated" as part of its own defense of imperialism.

This tug-of-war has not just started. It reached one climactic point at the Caracas Inter-American Conference where the U.S. sought to make "Communist infiltration" the main issue, twisting the arms of the Latin American delegates to get a majority vote for its resolution which was designed to lay the groundwork for possible intervention.

It has now reached another climax with the latest efforts of Washington to stir up a hue and cry about the "pro-Communist Guatemalan government" for buying arms from Czechoslovakia.

Even before the Caracas conference, there was common talk in the air about machinations by the State Department to use Honduras and Nicaragua, Guatemala's neighbors, as screens for intervention. The small Central American country which was the but of these maneuvers was meanwhile cut off from all arms purchases. Denied any military supplies from the U.S. and embargoed by U.S. influence, the Guatemalan government exercised its sovereign right to purchase arms from wherever it could get them — which was behind the Iron Curtain. In a blatant demonstration of "Yankee domination," Washington has had resort to open threats of force.

It is clear that this crude strong arm stuff has consolidated all elements in Guatemala — right, left and Stalinist — behind the Arbenz regime.

Here is how American imperialism demonstrates its invaluable aid to the growth of Stalinism in the Americas:

"Washington's outcry over this country's purchase of arms from Communist sources in Europe appears to have boomeranged," writes Sydney Gruson, N.Y. Times correspondent who is now back in Guatemala after having been expelled from it. "It has achieved. for Guatemala, a greater degree of national unity than she has experienced in a long time."

"Newspapers," he continues , "that normally are in constant opposition have rallied to the government's action in buying what the State Department described as an 'important shipment of arms' from Communist controlled territory. . . . "

(M   a   y   2   1   .   )

69

On May 24, Gruson wrote again:

The consensus here among Guatemalans and foreigners alike is that the United States has chosen the wrong issue in seeking a showdown with Guatemala over her purchase of arms behind the Iron Curtain.

For most Guatemalans the issue has thrust far into the background the question of whether the government of President Jacobo Arbenz Guzman is influenced or dominated by a Communist party dedicated to Moscow's ends. Friends and foes of the administration have closed ranks in support of the government's position that it had not only the right but a duty to buy arms wherever it could after the United States refused to sell it arms.

That this reaction should be shown so strongly by critics of the government has come as a shock to many. Guatemalans who had been crying for many months for the United States to do something about the political situation have joined the great upsurge of nationalism that has released itself against the United States since the arms issue arose.

If this was the "wrong issue," what was the "right" one? For, as we shall see, there *is* a way, a simple and obvious way, in which the United States can contribute to stem whatever dangers exist of Stalinist growth in Guatemala. But the *Times* correspondent's sources are not the ones who can put the finger on that. And so Gruson even admits that he (which means his American sources of opinion) do not know any "right" issue: "This [situation] has led many observers," he admits, "to wonder whether there could ever be an acceptable issue with which to try to stop the Communist advances in this country."

Let us quote Gruson further: "The reaction has served to remind observers that the dominant feeling among articulate Guatemalans is not pro or anticommunism or pro or anti-Yankeeism but fervent nationalism. It has been mirrored just as strongly in the independent press as in the government propaganda organs."

"Friends and foes" of the regime alike are being steeled to resist the U.S.'s disgraceful pressure, which is expected to come through some of the Inter-American Organization of the American States — economic or even military sanctions. They know that Washington could club enough of the member states into line if it got serious about using its economic weapons freely (the favorite weapons of American imperialism, since it became unfashionable to send the U.S. marines directly). But "in this event, they say, there would be great resentment against the United States in other countries." as Gruson reports — that is, an immediate "victory" might be won, but anti-American antagonism down south would only increase, opening the doors wider to Stalinist prestige, since the Stalinists would be put in the position of being the vanguard of defense of Latin American rights against the colossus of the North.

The power of the U.S. appears to be used against the Latin Americans with the same crude hypocrisy as characterizes Stalinist expansionism against its own victims. The common pattern is: the giant world power puts the squeeze on the small country; it resists; the giant thereupon begins to yell that its intended victim has "aggressive" intentions; the neighboring countries must be armed in "self defense"; under cover of this demagogy, intervention is prepared.

The rightist friends of Washington and United Fruit in Guatemala have been openly calling for organization of an anti-Arbenz camp by the U.S. In the current issue of the right wing *U.S. News & World Report,* an interview with two Guatemalan émigrés (now in Mexico) makes this clear, and the magazine publishes this interview with the sole purpose of plugging this course.

"When there are rats, you have to kill them. I am convinced ... that to exterminate it, there is just one route — gunpowder." This is the appeal by the émigrés which is presented.

"With respect to just what the United States can do," one of them states further, "I believe that nation has the duty of pulling the evil by its roots."

The Guatemalan people are not asking for an armed effort from any country. But they hope their leaders will be equipped in some effective way so that they can equip the people with war materials to accomplish the expulsion of those who have been guilty of treason by permitting foreign Communists to control the government — a practical intervention by Russia in Guatemala. I believe categorically that it is necessary to have a machine gun in order to take action against the arms brought from Russia. Someone has to give this help.

The U.S. has already taken steps to oblige. Planeloads of arms have been air lifted in a hurry to Honduras and Nicaragua, which have nice respectable governments, under obliging military dictatorships, who do not believe in inconveniencing United Fruit. The U.S. Coast Guard is threatening to stop any other ship laden with arms for Guatemala.

This isn't the first time that Honduras would be used in this way. 'Way back in 1933, *Fortune* magazine referred to these practices. In its March issue of that year it described the days when United Fruit was fighting the competition of Cuyamel Fruit company: "United Fruit, master of the Caribbean, considered Cuyamel a trespasser in Guatemala . . . So Guatemala protested to Honduras. Both countries sent troops into the valley and there were two or three skirmishes." (Two things have changed since then: United Fruit absorbed Cuyamel, thus ending that nuisance, and Guatemala is no longer a pliant tool.)

United Fruit is truly a master in the Caribbean. This trading octopus, based largely on Boston finance capital, is one of the big ten in foreign capital investments. At the end of 1948, it owned in Central America 558,965 acres of land; 1474 miles of railroad and 209 miles of other rail transportation; 72,082 head of livestock; 66 ocean vessels; the telegraph system linking the Caribbean countries with the U.S.; telephone lines, radio stations, sugar refineries, banana plantations, sugar plantations, etc.

With the Guatemalan government standing pat on its recent takeover of a part of the United Fruit Company lands, the United states stepped in as bill collector for its finance capitalists — a time honored role. One important fact behind the present crisis is the fact that the State Department intervened in a note to demand nearly 16 million dollars on behalf of United Fruit in compensation for the land, which was dealt with under Guatemala's agrarian reform law. Guatemala insists that United Fruit will be compensated but given no special treatment that is different from Guatemalan citizens affected by the law.

One cause of dispute is the fact that Guatemala wishes to compensate the company in accord with the valuation of the land on the basis of which the company has been taxed in the past. But now it turns out that this valuation, which was used for tax dodging, is too low in the eyes of the fruit emperors!

This bill collecting function of the U.S. government used to be exercised more frankly. The present generation may never have run across the classic exposé of this imperialist role which was famous in the 1930's. In the words of Major General Smedley D. Butler, describing his career as follows:

I spent 33 years and four months in active service as a member of our country's most agile military force — the Marine Corps. I served in all commissioned ranks from second lieutenant to major general. And during that period I spent most of my time being a high class muscle man for Big Business, for Wall Street, and for the bankers. In short I was a racketeer for capitalism. . . .

Thus, I helped make Mexico and especially Tampico safe for American oil interests in 1914. I helped make Haiti and Cuba a decent place for the National City Bank to collect revenues in . . . I helped purify Nicaragua for the international banking house of Brown Brothers in 1909-1912. I brought light to the Dominican Republic for American sugar interests in 1916. I helped make Honduras "right" for American fruit companies in 1903. In China in 1927 I helped see to it that Standard Oil went its way unmolested. (*Common Sense,* November 1935.)

Now the U.S. is trying to find a way in a world where anticolonialism is on the upsurge, to "democratize" Guatemala in 1954.

The United Fruit Company empire in the Caribbean is being pushed to the wall. It is not so much immediately concerned with the direct issue of Guatemalan expropriation as it is with the effect of such action on the rest of its empire. If Guatemala "gets away with it," how far behind will Costa Rica be? The strikers in Honduras will be encouraged. Other governments, now staying in line, will be emboldened, or, if they remain "loyal" to the master, will meet with greater and greater pressure at home because of their sellouts. There is more at stake for United Fruit than the interests in Guatemala alone.

And so the powerful United States accuses Guatemala of planning "aggression" — with a shipload of pistols and such. The N. Y. *Times* itself stated that "Foreign military observers described Guatemalan military equipment as 'antiquated' and badly in need of parts." If the recent shipment included more than light arms, they say, Guatemala would not even be able to assemble and operate them without help. (And no one claims to have spotted a Russian military mission there; there is only one military mission in the country — the American one.)

No responsible source claims that the Guatemalan Stalinists have yet succeeded in building up any genuine mass support. They are in *alliance* with the Arbenz regime, which is beset on all sides by enemies and seeks internal support on which to lean. That alliance can be broken, but it cannot be broken with any progressive results by external imperialist pressure. The later only feeds the sources of Stalinist strength.

The rug can be pulled from beneath Guatemalan Stalinism — from both the native Stalinist movement and from the hopes of the Moscow regime to use it as a base in the Western Hemisphere for propaganda and sabotage — only by removing the legitimate social issues on which it nourishes. As long as the U.S. dollar is the enemy of the people, the Stalinists can flourish — or else they can only be cut down by the type of brutal intervention, direct or indirect, which will merely aid them in the hemisphere as a whole.

It is the U.S. which is responsible for the growth and prospects of Stalinism in Guatemala. It is in this country that the remedy lies.

Washington can complain to Sweden for furnishing the ship which brought the arms to Puertos Barrios, but this only entangles it further with other countries which do not want to jump every time the State Department cracks the whip. Washington can complain to Britain on the ground that a British company is involved in the Swedish ship deal, but there is surely enough antagonism to the U.S. strong arm policy in Britain already. Washington can patrol the skies of Honduras with war planes — as the press reports it is doing now — but this will not drive the Honduran strikers back to labor in the banana plantations.

Washington can threaten an economic boycott of Guatemala — for example, an embargo on purchase of Guatemalan coffee — but this will get in the way of the U.S. coffee interests which need the high quality Guatemalan coffee to put some flavor in the Brazilian product (which is none too plentiful now anyway.)

Behind the present crisis with Guatemala is the fact that the U.S. is following an imperialist foreign policy in every field, not a democratic foreign policy. It talks about hemisphere democracy and other lofty subjects, but a capitalist government is a capitalist government.

It would be inaccurate to say that Guatemala could be the U.S.'s Indochina. Guatemala is not a political colony of this country. It would have to be a question of smashing its sovereignty in some way, or engineering the kind of internal coup which is supposed to be the peculiar talent of the Russian Stalinists but which is really an old story in the history of U.S. imperialism in Latin America.

Intervention, or provocation and subsidization of intervention, in Guatemala would be a high international crime. Stalinism can be defeated there too, as it can be defeated in Indochina, but the price to be paid for that is the downfall of imperialist interests.

There must be no intervention in Guatemala!

*   *   *

It has taken the imperialist liberals to strip the Guatemala issue down to its bare bone.

This is the dubious service performed by the editorial endorsement given by the New York *Post* to the Washington policy of supporting the reactionary rebels against the Guatemalan government.

Not even the N. Y. *Times*, we should note, rushed editorially to proclaim such endorsement. In fact, for two days running (June 20-21) *Times* editorials pretended that they didn't know what was really happening and would have to "withhold judgement," speaking of "confusion," "obscurity," "lack of information," etc.

Of course, we need have no doubts about the *Times'* loyalty to the American Party line, but its behavior at least bespeaks a formal recognition of certain copybook maxims about international democracy.

It does this in the same way that (for example) the government of Honduras bows to democratic principles when it lyingly *denies* its obvious complicity in the invasion-revolt. For if the Hondurans had bluntly admitted the truth, how callous that would prove them! A pretense of virtue is one of the last remnants of moral behavior to be shucked off by the vicious and the depraved.

But our liberals of the N. Y. *Post* — undoubtedly one of the most genuinely liberal papers in the country — will have no truck with such hypocrisy, not even in order to assuage their souls. They want to Face The Truth. They want to have NO Delusions. They want to Think It Through.

And in an important respect they do, even though, as we shall see, they do not quite succeed in Facing The Truth.

They think it right through to the principle, virtually proclaimed, that in the interests of its war against Russia, the U.S. can ride roughshod over the democratic rights of any other nation which refuses to line up (unspoken addendum: if it can get away with it.) They think it right through to the principle that in a "good" cause the U.S. has a right to do what it condemns on the part of the bad Russians.

Like virtually everybody else, the *Post* has often enough waxed indignant at the crimes of Moscow in suppressing small peoples, *properly using these acts to prove that Moscow's case must be bad.* But faced with a crime by its own government, our liberals stand their own thinking on end; the same, or at least fatally similar, acts by the U.S. are justified on the ground that these crimes are directed to a good cause. We will not pursue this into the question of "means and ends" that liberal pundits so delight in discussing when they are explaining the sins of the Bolsheviks.

No, the *Post* will not be hypocritical and it admits with some asperity that "We [by which it means not itself but the U.S. government] have plainly encouraged the rebels, and we render ourselves a trifle ludicrous by joining in a solemn call for a 'ceasefire' as they start marching."

But the Post's basic justification is that Guatemala is CP-dominated and that therefore anything goes.

And yet, although it must make this claim in order to make its point, it does *not* quite make this claim but only insinuates it.

Because, of course, there is not a single responsible observer who has been able to show that Guatemala is decisively *dominated* by the CP in any real sense. The facts amply prove the influence of the CP, the government's toleration and aid to the CP, etc., but they do not go even halfway to proving what the *Post* must prove if its argument is to reach even first base: and that is CP domination and nothing else.

Unless, of course, our liberals are also prepared to argue that a small country must be crushed even if there is only a danger that the CP may dominate some time in the future!

How does the *Post* editorial present this factual question? Our liberals, who insist on being so honest, edge up to it like guilty men, with the following series of verbal approximations:

. . . the Arbenz government has *steadily succumbed to Communist pressure;*

. . . real Communists were *doing real business* in Guatemala;

. . . it was the Communist movement which was *gaining* the ascendancy;

. . . Arbenz chose to make a *deal* with the Communists;

. . . the underlying sham is the Russian claim that the Communist drive in Guatemala is *independent of Moscow;*

. . . Arbenz was letting the Communists assume *dominance* in his regime;

. . . this *Soviet base* of operations;

. . . the central fact was *Russian intervention* on this continent.

And the liberal conclusion is that "in the real world it was inconceivable that the U.S. would — or should — remain indifferent to this Soviet base of operations.

"We are committed to the rebels," proclaims the Post. This is its understanding of how liberals must live "in the real world."

Thus our liberals endorse the Dulles principle that a "Communist government" cannot be tolerated anywhere even if established legally, democratically, and with the will of the people. This is also the principle which the British established in the case of British Guiana. It is an open repudiation of their claim that Stalinism's crime is to impose its will *over* people's necks.

The *Post* must endorse this principle because its basic argument, so "courageously" faced, points to it inescapably. If Guatemala must be crushed, because a CP is too influential in its government circles — a government, moreover, which has been one of the more democratic in Latin America, relatively speaking, and not among the dictatorships that are Washington's pets — certainly any country must be crushed as soon as the CP becomes dominant legally.

But if the U.S. can crush a country in which its imperialist rival is too influential — by what right do our liberals condemn the Russians for doing the same thing?

Do not the Russians have the right to feel endangered when the U.S. builds up armies, and establishes bases, on its very flanks? Do not the Russians have the right to crush any neighboring country (if *they* can get away with it) which is being used by the U.S. as a war jumpoff point?

There is Iran on the Russian flank. There is Turkey. No one in the world is uncertain as to whether these regimes do not represent a dagger pointed at Russia. And there was Korea ...

This is exactly the pro-Stalinist, apologetic, or merely "neutralist" thinking, of so many elements in Europe and Asia: we cannot condemn the Russians, for their crimes, they say, because the poor Russians are afraid and encircled ...

We Independent Socialists will have no truck with this apologetic or "neutralist" whitewash of the Kremlin. But our liberals, who are even more bitter about such talk? Do they not agree completely with these apologists of oppression, except that they are willing to whitewash only *the U.S. camp and vilify the rival war camp?*

Our liberals of *Post* caliber want to live "in the real world" and they are willing to go along with an international crime (swallowed hard and painfully) because it is simply inconceivable for them that Guatemala should be allowed to go its own way. *Why?* Why — even if we grant what is not true, that Guatemala is already controlled by the Stalinists?

Taking it only on the most immediate plane, why is it that these good liberals of ours cannot even take such a calmer view as that of the *Times'* military analyst Hanson Baldwin, who might have been exposing the *Post* type liberals when he wrote the following passage:

The dimensions of the Guatemalan military force indicate that it cannot possibly be taken as a serious threat to United States interests — though ,under a Communist government, a peasant army of considerable size that would be capable of overawing neighboring states might be formed in time.

Nor does Guatemala's geographic position constitute too serious a threat. The capital is 840 air miles from the Panama Canal, and Communist airfields hacked out of the jungle could pose a potential threat to the Canal. But the concealment of such airfields and their construction could not be hidden, and the Canal itself, though important economically and logistically, no longer is the vital lifeline it was prior to the age of air power.

The public importance attached to the Guatemalan situation, therefore, is disproportionate to Guatemalan military capabilities. Yet, in the overall context of strategy, the problem deserves the attention it is getting though it cannot be solved by the means so far employed. In fact, the military elements of what is essentially a political, economic and ideological problem have been greatly overstressed, with results that already are reacting against the United States.

Even if a "Communist" Guatemala would be a more serious difficulty than Baldwin makes out, why does that justify a Moscow type suppression? Russia has been forced to live with a ring of hostile bases for years. Can the U.S. not stand a single "beachhead" of the enemy in an insignificantly weak country which is itself ringed by U.S. satellites?

We can easily understand that this is enough to panic a Dulles, an Eisenhower, even a Truman, into action which parallels Russia's: *what exactly is it that has panicked our liberals?* Why, in the editorial under discussion, did every prop of democratic thinking and moral internationalism collapse in their minds like papier-maché?

But these are "immediate" considerations. We are willing to Think It Through further. What if the threat were even more serious than is presently represented by Guatemala?

Anyone who starts thinking along these lines — hypothetical ones, we emphasize — cannot avoid posing the whole question in an entirely different manner than the purely imperialist framework in which the Post *editorialist is caught.*

Stalinism can become such a danger, even hypothetically, only because it feeds on, and grows on, the crimes of the capitalist imperialism, on the hatred of the peoples for U.S. overlordship and national brutality.

Stalinism can get to the point of even posing the problem in the fashion feared by our liberals only because of the inability of capitalist imperialism to offer the people an alternative they can live with.

And while Stalinism grows on the brutality of imperialism — and this is the lesson of our era which overshadows every other one without exception — our liberals propose to support that imperialist brutality in the name of defeating Stalinism!

That is the basic error made by liberals who reluctantly, and with much heartburning, feel that they have to go along with imperialism in order to live in the "real world."

They are living in a delusion, in a dream.

That dreamlike quality comes right out in the *Post* editorial itself. It ends by raising the question whether the rebels, to whom it is committed, aim only at "a cold-blooded military adventure which ends in destroying the limited economic reforms that poverty-drenched Guatemala has achieved." Do they fly the flag of United Fruit or of freedom, it asks.

Come, come, gentlemen of the *Post*; we know you want to show that your heart is in the right place, but leave us not be mushbrained about it all. If you want to be hardheaded and live in the real world, as you say, then go ahead; but with a minimum of silliness. The army which Washington is supporting (with the not valueless additional support of the *Post*) is the armed force of the landlords who want to destroy the agrarian reform, of the bosses and hangers on of United Fruit and the coffee *finqueros* who long for the good old days before this pestiferous Guatemalan revolution started. Overthrow of the Arbenz regime will mean a reign of bloody terror by these elements not only against the CPers but against the far more numerous nationalists of all stripes who supported the Arbenz social program. The center of gravity of Guatemalan politics will inescapably swing far to the right.

Face it, dear liberals. You can't have your revolution and crush it too.

In your own way — little or big, with the best of liberal intentions and not at all as part of a deep-dyed imperialist "plot" — you will thus educate all the world that it is only the Stalinists, for all their own horrors, who can consistently support movements of social progress against landlordism and colonialism. You will rightly explain, no doubt, that the Stalinists bring worse evils in their train, but you will show in life and not in words that you attack Stalinist crimes only in order to reconcile the peoples to capitalist-imperialist crimes. And they will not be reconciled.

They will not cease fighting. They will not take your advice to be good and bow the head to United Fruit because of the necessity of defeating Russia somewhere else in the world. You cannot make them live in that world, because it is not the "real world" of their misery and poverty.

You cannot make them think like an American liberal any more than — much of the time — you can even succeed in thinking like liberals yourselves.

It is American imperialism, and basically nothing else, which is responsible for the growth of Stalinism in Guatemala. Because you cannot bring yourself to oppose American imperialism, when the chips are down, you are among those greasing the road for Stalinism.

Labor Action
June 7,28

In the fall of 1955 the Independent Socialist League participated in a Third Camp conference along with some pacifist groups, on the basis of the watchword "Neither Washington nor Moscow!" At this conference, someone *gave a report on what was happening on Okinawa under American control - I regret to say I cannot remember who performed this service. It woke me up to an embarrassing fact: American socialists, such as they were, had never paid much attention to the peoples who were* directly *controlled by their government. Certainly* Labor Action *had not done so, and it was little consolation to find, when I scouted around, that no one else had done so either. I thought that was a shameful state of affairs by neglect, or by ommission rather than commission, and set about recruiting writers to do a research job. This recruitment was only partially successful, and I wound up doing most of the job myself. (Incidentally, the case of Puerto Rico is* not *included in these strictures:* Labor Action *had paid a good deal of attention to that island, especially with the help of Ruth Reynolds - a pacifist, not a socialist - who was a supporter of the Nationalist group.)*

We were well aware that Okinawa, Samoa and Guam were small places with few people; but without inflating the issue at all, this was a case where one had to say: "It's the principle of the thing." I was rocked back on my heels one day after we had advertised the scheduled article on Samoa: "Who cares about that stuff? What difference does it make?" *gritted a self-styled socialist, meaning that he didn't see why we, who had such important world affairs to discuss, should waste space on these inconsequential bits of territory. I would gladly have voted for his expulsion, except that I was opposed to expulsion on grounds of stupidity. Instead I gave the Samoan article the title it bears: "Who Cares About Samoa?" But when I think of the fate of the socialist movement I remember that person . . .*

H. D.

The Crime of Okinawa

American Bulldozers at Work
On the "Cyprus of the Pacific"

As this study of the U.S. crime of Okinawa was being prepared Secretary
of State Dulles reached Tokyo on march 18 in the course of his world
perambulation and was greeted, among other ways, by a demonstration
demanding the liberation of Okinawa. That made one sentence in an inside-
page N. Y. *Times* dispatch which was headlined "Dulles Broadcasts to North
Korea That Liberation Is Firm U.S. Goal."

It is no doubt the firm goal of U.S. power to "liberate" the possessions of
all its enemies. This is equally the firm goal of the world Stalinist power,
which thereby achieves an "anti-imperialist" reputation among some.

*But the test of a genuine democrat is that he fights for the freedom of peoples oppressed
by his own government, without compromising his denunciation of oppression anywhere.*

By this standard, U.S. democracy is cankered. There are few spots on earth
where the toll of imperialist domination has been as heavy on a people as it
has been in Okinawa under American occupation. Yet who is even aware of
it in this country?

In the same issue of the *Times* above-mentioned, the resistance in Cyprus
to British military terror was on the front page. Yet - leaving aside the obvious
difference that the people of Cyprus are now fighting militantly, while the
people of Okinawa are still protesting peacefully - there is a striking similarity
between the cases of the two islands.

Both are held by foreign powers who insist on hanging on to their rule on
the plea of military "security" - their own military security, of course, not that
of the islanders.

In both cases the overwhelming majority of the islanders demand union
with another country (Okinawa with Japan.)

If there is a difference, it is that the Okinawans have far more immediate
reason to wish freedom from the U.S.'s grasp, even apart from nationalist
considerations.

*Yet hundreds of thousands of words of justified sympathy are being poured out in this
country on behalf of the Cypriots, but the case of the Okinawans is blacked out.*

Is it because there are only a handful of people involved? - No, there are a million
subjugated people in the Ryukyu Islands; and the 600,000 on Okinawa alone
number far more than the whole population of Cyprus.

Is it that "we" are entitled to rule Okinawa because "we" liberated her in the war against Japan? Didn't our GI's give their lives on its shores? etc. - Then Russia is entitled to rule Eastern Europe. Indeed, Russian troops *did* help to liberate its present satellites from a Nazi occupation that the people hated, whereas U.S. troops did *not* "liberate" the Okinawan people when they seized it as a military objective.

Or is the freedom of the Okinawans of such lesser interest to our great democrats because its people are not members of the white race?

The Air-Conditioned Nightmare

In any case, here is the truth about what the United States has done in the only land which is today directly under its own military occupation.

The people of Okinawa are not Japanese and do not consider themselves Japanese. They are Okinawans.

They are a people with their own proud history, culture and way of life., which the United States is now engaged in destroying with brutal methods. If they wish union with Japan, it is because for several centuries now Japanese influence has been dominant and effective in determining the orientation of the people.

From the 14th into the 17th century Chinese influence was uppermost, under the Ming dynasty, but never achieved real governmental domination of the Ryukyu island group. Japanese influence began in the first years of the 17th century. By 1879 it was incorporated into the Japanese empire, the native king becoming a Japanese peer. The process did not differ that much from the transformation within Japan proper, of other feudal states into the centralized government under the restored Meiji emperor. It was not the kind of colonial conquest that characterized the formation of the European empires.

Today, the Okinawans almost universally speak Japanese as fluently as their native Ryukyuan language, and "many of their characteristics are Japanese." [1]

The Okinawans are not the savages who generally, in the American popular mind, populate the Pacific islands. We point this out somewhat apologetically, since we do not wish to imply that it would be all right to oppress savages. It is still important to note that this people whose home has been taken away from them are, and long have been, a highly cultured people.

The Ryukyu Islanders have a higher literacy rate than the great United States of America. [2]

The editors of the *Christian Century*, who pointed this out in one editorial, said in another: "Okinawans are not primitive South Sea islanders. They had achieved a high degree of civilization when Scotsmen were still eating each other. Their poets, dramatists and composers antedate those of the British Isles. Their musical dramas, some of them of operatic caliber, are a highly developed art form." [3]

War-Torn Island

This is the people who were caught up in the Second World War, and today the name Okinawa mainly denotes to Americans the scene of a great Pacific battle. What was merely a battlefield to the contending U.S. and Japanese forces was - their home.

"So savage were the bombardments that Okinawa was altered almost beyond recognition...all the large towns and villages had to be rebuilt from scratch. At least 50,000 Okinawan civilians were killed or seriously wounded." [4] Another source speaks of the "Complete destruction of the two cities of Shuri and Naha [the capital] and of about 90 percent of the rest of the island ..." [5] And "almost anyone visiting Okinawa today, five years after the end of the war in asia, would get the impression that some terrible scourge had descended upon and remained with both islands and people. Certainly it must seem so to the Okinawans themselves..." [6]

But what the war itself did to Okinawa is not our theme.* Other lands suffered as battlefields too, in the fury of the world-wide slaughter, though few in as concentrated a fashion. It is simply the background of what has happened since.

Grabbed From Japan

In the first place, the islands were detached from Japan without the victorious powers even bothering to invent a moral-sounding reason. The official rationale would seem to be the Cairo declaration of December 1943: "Japan will also be expelled from all other territories she has taken by violence

---

* But one should not ignore the following incident: "The physician who is in charge of the Airakuen leper colony told ... that the colony has few badly crippled lepers because all such died in 1945-46. Mistaking it for a Japanese army installation our planes blasted and strafed the leper colony and burned it to the ground. The lepers took to their caves and only one was wounded. But 300 died of starvation." (*Christian Century,* January 23, 1952.)

and greed," which certainly does not apply to Okinawa as long as the people themselves demand return. The Potsdam declaration of 1945 reaffirmed the statement but nowhere are the Ryukyu mentioned by name. The peace treaty stated explicitly that the U.S. would exercise immediate complete control over the islands but gives no reason. [7]

The reason, of course, is simply that the Truman government wanted it so, to build the islands into its own fortress. This was why they were not even formally over to UN trusteeship.

Japan even remains the "technical" owner of the islands, though this fact is mainly a juridical curiosity. It underlines, however, the enormity of what the U.S. is doing with utter callousness to a land which it does not even "own" in the imperialist sense.

There is not the slightest doubt that, as we have reported, the mass of Okinawans desire return to Japan, as well as that the Japanese demand this reunification. The latest to confirm this is the American Civil Liberties Union, in its statement last year to the Defense Department on civil rights in Okinawa: "the major agitation in Okinawa, the Union said, is for reversion of the island to its former status as part of Japan, which practically all of the natives desire." [8]

In the 1954 legislative elections on the island, "The Socialist Party, favoring the return of Okinawa to Japan, won the largest single vote . . . the U.S. army said today," reported the *Times.* [9]

There is also a relatively weak tendency that wants independence, and another that favors UN trusteeship under the U.S. It can be imagined what sort of native quislings could possibly favor the status quo under the U.S. army as today; we shall mention them later on.

(Japan, of course, is officially on record as demanding the return of Okinawa. in July 1953 a unanimous resolution of the Japanese lower house, supported by all political parties, called on the government to take prompt action for its restoration.)

But Washington has made it clear that, whoever is supposed to own Okinawa, it will never give it up, either to Japan or Okinawa. This is taken for granted by everyone, however official or unofficial, who has ever mentioned the subject. It was made virtually official by a Dulles statement, made as a 1953 Christmas Day present to the Okinawans, asserting that "the U.S. intends to remain as custodian of these Islands for the foreseeable future." [10]

On this occasion the U.S. returned the Amamis Islands but Dulles said it was holding on to Okinawa "until conditions of genuine stability and confidence are created" - i.e. until the cows ome home.

One hundred years after Commodore Perry had proposed, in his own *italics* that the strategic islands be put under the "*surveillance* of the American Flag *upon the ground of relamation for insults and injuries committed upon Americn Citizens*" (the best excuse the pious chap could think of so early in the days of U.S. imperialism); one hundred years after Perry called for their occupation in accordance with the "strictest rules of moral law" and the "laws of stern necessity," [11] The Ryukyus were indeed and at long last put into the hands of the occidental imperialists by the Japanese peace treaty.

Base for Empire

The century-old reason why Okinawa has beeen tempting an American land-grab is its strategic position in the Pacific - not in some special sense for defense of the U.S. but for domination of the Far East.

Reference Notes

1. T.T. Brumbaugh, "'God-Forsaken' Okinawa," *Christian Century,* June 7, 1950.

2. "Okinawa - Five Years After," *Christian Century,* January 23, 1952.

3. "If Okinawa Is Not To Be 'God-Forsaken'," *Christian Century,* August 16, 1950.

4. Demaree Rees, "Okinawa-American Island," *Saturday Evening Post,* July 11, 1953.

5. "If Okinawa Is Not To Be God-Forsaken"

6. "God-Forsaken Okinawa."

7. Ralph Braibanti, "The Ryukyu Islands: Pawn of the Pacific," *American Political Science Review,* December 1954.

8. ACLU *Weekly Bulletin.* October 31, 1955, summarizing ACLU proposals to Defense Department by Roger Baldwin, based on a review of material submitted by Japanese Federation of Bar Associations, Japan Civil Liberties Union, and Okinawan Residents' Association.

9. N. Y. *Times,* April 1, 1954

10. N. Y. *Times,* December 25, 1953.

11. In his dispatch from Okinawa on January 12, 1954.

Guam

Island on Your Conscience

The coolie wage issue which we have described for American Samoa also applies to Guam, but there the situation is worse and more complex. For one thing it is not so much a question of the native Guamanians, who have their own problems, as of a specially imported coolie labor force — Filipinos.

Here too the dollar minimum wage of the States is supposed to apply. But the law has not been enforced, and the government has no intention to enforce it.

Instead, bills were presented in the last Congress to cover up the violation of the law, by (1) giving the secretary of Labor power to supersede the Fair Labor Standards Act with his own setting of the minimum wage scale, and (2) exempting employers *retroactively* from their liability for the back wages that they should have been paying in accordance with the law.

Here the coolie labor system is on a much bigger scale than in Samoa. Guam is an important navy base, with considerable navy construction and other work going on, much of it through private contractors (U.S. companies).

There are over 10,000 Filipino workers that have been brought over to Guam (Philippine Ambassador Romulo gives the figure of 13,000 for both Guam and Wake Island). Over 7000 are working on navy contracts; the air force employs about 1500 more; and 2000 work for private employers.

In 1947 Washington and Manila exchanged notes agreeing on terms by which U.S. contracting firms could recruit Filipino workers for Guam. The attraction is that a Filipino can earn more on Guam that he can from the wages available in the depressed conditions of his own country.

But this "more" — counting in allowance for benefits — is only from 53 to 57 cents an hour! A Filipino may get 75 cents an hour in a job that would pay an American craftsman at his elbow $3 an hour for the same work.

But, as we have explained in the case of Samoa, it is flatly illegal to pay this pittance to workers in American territory.

Everybody including the government admits it is illegal. In fact, the employers, government representatives and investigating congressmen are all equally afraid that "some bright lawyer" might sue on behalf of the workers — and collect millions.

Moreover, at this last session of Congress Guam (unlike Samoa) was *not* exempted from the minimum wage. So it still legally applies. But there is no more intention of enforcing it than before, as far as the eye can see.

On Guam, moreover, it is the government itself that would have to pay up if the *contractors* are found by a court to be liable for the back wages which they have been keeping from their coolies (estimated at $3 million). This is so because of a provision in the contracts. So the contractors are sitting pretty, but the Defense Department is in a sweat to get out from under by pushing the proposed legislation through Congress.

Of the proposal for *retroactive* exemption from the minimum wage, the AFL-CIO's legislative representative Walter J. Mason told the congressional committee last February 28:

> [This provision] which would give retroactive immunity to past violators of the law could establish an extremely dangerous precedent. Congress should not now deprive workers of the wages which they were entitled to receive at a time when the Fair Labor Standards Act fully applied to them. Any employer who failed to comply with the law did so in full knowledge that the law applied to him.

Now there is no doubt that this is true. It was openly put on the record of the hearing committee.

A Defense Department lawyer pointed out that in some other cases the government might get off the hook by telling a court there was a mixup in "good faith," but in the case of Guam — "In my opinion, gentlemen, it would be extremely difficult to establish a `good-faith' defense that would get us out of that retroactive liability. . . . Because of the obvious geographic application of the act by its own terms, it would be very difficult to argue that there was no knowledge that the act did apply."

Incredible as it may seem, this is not pointed out by the government lawyers to show that the violation of the law must stop — *this thought, literally never came up from any government quarter at any of the sessions!* — but only to show why the law has to be changed.

The Labor Department admitted that it had never even set up the most elementary machinery to check labor conditions in Guam, let alone enforce the law. Its representative Lundquist told of his ignorance as to the wages paid.

CONGRESSMAN ELLIOTT: "The truth is the Wage and Hour Division of the Department of Labor does not have any facilities by which to enforce the application of this act in most of the areas that you mentioned here [U.S. possessions]. And, furthermore, it does not even have the facilities to learn whether or not the local people are paying the 75-cent minimum [now $1], or, as a matter of fact, it does not know what is being paid in most of these areas. Is that not true when you get right down to the administration of the act?"

LUNDQUIST: "We have no field offices, no investigators in those areas. That is correct."

Guam is an excellent example of how labor laws on the books mean little unless there is an organized labor movement to enforce them. The passage of social legislation does not supersede the class struggle.

A procession of administration officers appeared before the committee to plead against the minimum wage for Guam: from State, Interior, Labor and Defense; and in the latter case from all three arms, navy, army, and air force. All kinds of pretexts were given for keeping wages at the coolie level.

Prominent was the one we discussed in the case of Samoa: one should not "disrupt" the economies of neighboring areas that are affected by developments in the U.S. territory. Admiral Parks for the navy even directly cited the case of Morocco, where French capital bitterly opposed the paying of high U.S. wages because this "spoils" the natives for the lower-paying French exploiters.

Making this argument in the case of Guam, however, can only have reference to the Philippines, the home of the coolie labor supply. But as we shall see, the Philippine government and that whole country squarely backed the dollar wage for its citizens.

The tender solicitude which the American officials expressed lest they "disrupt" Guam or the Philippines with higher wages awakes no answering echo of gratitude in the Guamanians or Filipinos who are being saved from the appalling danger of being paid a dollar an hour.

The military gentlemen had a second and more honest motivation to explain: the workers must continue to get coolie wages in order to save money for the Defense Department budget. As Admiral Parks said, "we are principally interested in the Department of Defense in stretching the defense dollars as far as they will go."

This motivation we can believe, but then two questions arise: (1) Why all the twaddle about rescuing the natives from the horrors of a dollar wage that would "disrupt" their economy? (2) Wouldn't this motivation also justify wage cutting the U.S. itself, *if they could get away with it?*

The following colloquy took place:

> *REP. LANDRUM:* (D. Ga.): "So, by the use of the amount of Guamanian labor that you can employ and by the use of these Filipinos which [*sic*] you have brought in there, you are . . . saving the American taxpayers at least $30 million per year?"

> *ADMIRAL PARKS:* "Yes, sir."

> *LANDRUM:* "Now, then, the only reason being advanced presently for increasing the expenditure of the American taxpayers in order to maintain this is to quiet the alleged propaganda from some of our enemies that we are failing to pay standard wages for labor being done on American soil. Is that right?"

> *PARKS*: "That is as I understand it, sir."

> *LANDRUM*: "My own opinion is that I am getting tired of spending money every time somebody pinches me in the seat to turn around and give them another dollar."

This Southern intellect might have continued in this statesmanlike vein, but James Roosevelt interrupted to say, "I am well persuaded by your argument," but would the Defense Department object if the wage restrictions were lifted only on "defense work"?

Parks said that would be all right with the Defense Department. But it was pointed out that the bills as drawn make no such distinction, and could establish Guam as a haven for runaway sweatshops.

In any case (unlike the French in the case of Morocco) it was precisely the Philippine government that has fought against the proposed bills to continue the coolie status of Filipino workers and others on Guam. This may have been the main reason why Guam was not finally included in the bills when they were passed by Congress.

The Philippine ambassador Carlos P. Romulo wrote in a letter that the exemption of the Filipino workers on the islands from the minimum wage law "will be an act of discrimination against them," and he added ominously: "the implications that will be drawn by the peoples of Asia from such legislation are of such far reaching significance" that one had to understand it.

In an official protest to Dulles, Romulo stressed that "what we are really asking for in their [Filipino workers'] behalf is but the righting of an injustice simply by enforcing an already existing law."

And he said diplomatically: "We must not give the enemies of democracy and freedom an opportunity to distort America's motives and magnify the amendment as a desire of the United States to perpetuate what they will undoubtedly brand as coolie labor."

It was this kind of talk that Landrum regarded as a pinch in the seat. To counter Romulo, some State Department troops were brought into the hearing.

One striped-pants commando was Daniel Goott, the department's specialist on international labor affairs, who blandly testified that passage of the bills could *not* cause any "adverse repercussions abroad" for the simple reason that they do not change "what is already in existence, that is, from a practical standpoint." In other words, since the wage law is violated anyway, passing a law to kill it should not bother anybody.

A second State Department man, Philip Sullivan (Far Eastern Affairs), at least admitted there was a problem, if only because of "the publicity which the papers in the Philippines are giving" to the issue ("the press was full of it"). His contribution was to argue that the bill was not discriminatory as charged because it applied to everybody, not only Filipinos — that is, it permitted Americans also to be paid coolie wages — as if any American would sign up for labor in Guam at 57 cents an hour!

Admiral Parks let slip one reason why the government was so anxious to get Guam removed from minimum wage coverage. The Philippine government, he explained, has asked for negotiations to revise the 1947 agreements; he wanted Congress to act on the bill urgently "because, frankly, it will strengthen our hands in negotiations with the Philippine government."

Right now, wouldn't it be embarrassing for State Department negotiators to try to argue Philippine negotiators into an agreement which constituted an open and admitted flouting of the U.S. law?

Yet it is important for Washington to beat down Manila's demands. As the Chief of Naval Operations put it bluntly, in a letter in the record on the forthcoming Philippine negotiations: "A departure from the practice of setting wages based upon those prevailing in an overseas area, for which the Philippine government appears to be pressing, could cause a chain reaction affecting other departments which employ non-U.S. citizens in overseas areas."

That is, the coolie wage system must not be cracked at any point, lest it all be swept away by a "chain reaction" of workers' discontent.

The Philippine Trade Union Council also protested "this class legislation" and asked the AFL-CIO "to counteract the reactionary and discriminatory measure."

The AFL-CIO representative Mason followed up with vigorous opposition to the bill. It was discriminatory . . . class legislation which would establish wage discrimination based on color, race or creed." It was "disappointing" that the first concern of the congressional committee was not to extend the coverage of the wage act to more workers, but was rather to remove workers from its protection. It "would simply feed grist to the mills of the Communist propaganda machine . . . blemish our record as a trustee of people in an underdeveloped area."

He also proposed that *if* the islands were to be exempted from the wage act, then the setting of the local minimum wage should not be left simply to the Secretary of Labor's say-so but should be done, as in the Virgin Islands, by a tripartite commission (industry, labor, government).

In the midst of the congressional hearings, the Guam legislature itself adopted a resolution protesting the exclusion of Guam from the dollar minimum wage coverage. This leads us into the second part of this situation — the interest of the Guamanians themselves in the matter as distinct from the interest of, or on behalf of, the imported Filipinos.

The population of Guam is over 35,000, of whom 30,803 are local citizens (Guamanians proper). There are over 2700 statesiders resident on the island. (In addition, there are the
10 — 11,000 Filipinos whom we have discussed.)

In the Guamanians we have a people who have been far more thoroughly assimilated into Western culture than the Samoans. This process was accomplished in large part by the mailed fist, under Spanish rule. It is a very interesting history which we cannot go into here; suffice to say Guam presents a classic case of conversion to civilization through the combined compulsions of cannon and cross. The native Chamorro culture was stamped out with gunpowder and holy water.

But from the massacres and suffering of the past, the Guamanian people have emerged as a people widely respected for ability, intelligence, skills and modernity in outlook. They are no Pacific primitives but well-qualified

American citizens. Their economic, social and political problems are eminently *modern* ones too.

In the background is a high cost-economy based on imported necessities, because any other means of subsistence has been destroyed by the civilizers and nothing put in place except a highly militarized economy. This is no South Seas Island where the natives can live on coconuts. The cost of living in Guam is higher than in the States, because practically all food, clothing, building materials, household stuff and commercial mechanical equipment have to be brought in by ocean shipment.

Guam legislator Cynthia Torres, testifying in Washington, told the congressional committee:

If the present way of life in Guam is to continue, the annual cash income of the head of the family must be $3000 and this is difficult of attainment even should the minimum wage provided by the Fair Labor Standards Act be continued and enforced." She quoted the last cost of living survey in Guam: "The estimated total value of purchases of the average family in Guam . . . is $2970.37 . . . ."

Now it developed at the hearings that the majority of the Guamanians are already getting the U.S. minimum wage, unlike the Filipinos. What then were the Guamanian representatives, Cynthia Torres and Won Pat, complaining about? They ably explained why the mass of coolie labor in the island depressed the conditions of the Guamanians too.

For one thing, a minor point, if the Filipino laborers on the island got higher wages, they would have more to spend, the extra amounts going to fatten the Guamanian economy, which needed it badly.

For another, Cynthia Torres pointed out, if the wages of one group (the Filipinos) working for the federal government were set by the secretary of Labor at a low level, this would give Guamanian businessmen a lever to push down their own workers' wages.

The Guamanian representatives argued that Guamanians, as U.S. citizens who pay taxes according to the laws of the U.S. should receive all the benefits of other laws free from discrimination.

But most important was the fact that the use of cheap Filipino labor was causing unemployment for the more expensive Guamanian labor. The resolution of the Guam legislature referred to "over 3000 American citizens over 18 years of age who are not now gainfully employed." Every year another 500 were added to the potential labor supply.

One reason why these Guamanians were not employed by the navy or other government agencies was simply that the Filipinos were cheaper. The government preferred to train Filipino workers than Guamanian. (Then it cited the Guamanians' lack of training as a reason for not hiring them!)

On this question of Guamanian unemployment, the testimony of the Hon. Ford Q. Elvidge, governor of Guam, presented the honorable governor as a broken-field runner of no mean dodging ability.

He began with the claim that "as a matter of fact, almost everybody on Guam who is employable today can get or has a job." A well paying job? He didn't say. Are there no unemployed? Under questioning he said first, "I do not know what is meant by the word unemployed," but in the same breath he asserted there are "very few." Pressed further, he admitted he had no figures. Could he even estimate? "I would not be able to estimate that number." Then he retreated to the formulation that "unemployment on Guam is today at a minimum. . . ." After some more squirming he protested, "I just would not be able to put a number on it."

The same Hon. Ford Q. Elvidge was much more definite when it came to explaining why he was so anxious to save the Guamanian people from the operation of the dollar minimum wage.

Why would this be bad for Guam? "To require employers to pay a minimum of $1 per hour might cause employers to recruit more expensive but higher skilled labor from Hawaii or the mainland, rather than pay a higher wage to less skilled local labor." This sort of argument may convince some Guamanians that if the U.S. government cannot protect their interests they need a sufficient degree of autonomy to take their own fate in their hands.

As Won Pat said, "Since in federal areas the Legislature of Guam has no jurisdiction over wages or conditions of work, we are not able to protect our people. . . ."

Besides, it developed, the leading government contractor on the island followed racist employment practices in refusing to hire Guamanians!

This was the Brown-Pacific-Maxon Construction Company, which reputedly handles about 90 per cent of the military construction jobs on the island.

A Guamanian legislator, J. T. Sablan, was the first to refer to this at the hearings.

"The BPM Construction Co. is a company somewhat owned or controlled by Southerners, and they do not want to hire people other than Caucasians, and the reason why they have Filipinos is because they give them a slave or low salary. Now as proof of that, I don't think there is a single Negro in that unit," he said on the record.

The governor, the Hon. Fred Q. himself, admitted that "it is my understanding they do not hire Guamanians" but almost exclusively Filipinos" (outside of the better paying jobs reserved for white statesiders).

Won Pat of the Guam legislature affirmed that BPM not only refused to hire Guamanians but also would not hire statesiders "who happen to marry a Guamanian."

"Well, it is easy to understand," he added, in answer to a question. "These aliens [Filipinos] are paid what we call in common terminology coolie wages or slave wages . . . and in addition I will say that since they are aliens they will be more submissive to the employer's wishes."

BPM, said Cynthia Torres, has steadfastly refused even to answer letters from the Guam Legislature addressed to them on this matter. (But that Southern statesman, Rep. Landrum, objected to using the word discrimination to describe BPM's policy: "they want to employ some other labor instead of the Guamanians," that's all, he explained.)

It should be added that BPM, it was testified, is an open shop outfit — as is also a second big contracting firm, Vinnell. There are no labor unions on Guam, Won Pat told the committee; "It is difficult to organize labor on Guam because most of them are working for the government."

Racism, open shoppism, discrimination, antiunionism, coolie wages and unemployment — here are some the distinctive features of an economy forced on the Guamanian people by the American military government's policies.

But the Guam Legislature's representatives also raised more basic questions about what the U.S. has done to the island's economy and the longer range interests of the people. Here is the gist of it, in Won Pat's exposition:

Guam has a payroll economy. It is based on expenditures, largely military, made necessary by maintaining Guam as a military base. Guam has little valuable mineral resources and therefore no mining industry. Its manufacturing industry is very limited. There is no lumber industry and no exports except a small amount of copra and scrap metal. Only about 700 people make their living in whole or in part

99

from agriculture. With the exception of some poultry-raising and egg-producing enterprises, as well as truck farming, we have no commercial agriculture in Guam. There are no food canneries or food processing plants. The military and residents depend largely on imported food. In addition we import all our clothes, all our home furnishings and appliances, and most of our building material from the mainland . . . paid for at mainland prices plus transportation and other costs.

Now what this describes is an economy that has been completely distorted for the benefit of the master and regardless of the long range interests of the Guamanian people.

Guam is being made unviable *except* as a military camp follower.

The land has been taken away by the military, even more than in Okinawa. Before the war Guam's economy was traditionally agricultural; money economy was minor. But this changed with the reoccupation of the island in 1944.

The U.S. government owns 32.78 per cent of all land in Guam, and holds another 3.73 per cent under leasehold control — over 36 per cent. The Government of Guam owns 22.94 per cent. It is understandable, explained Won Pat, why we have a payroll-military economy and no commercial agriculture, "for included in the 36 percent of lands owned or controlled by the military is a majority of the finest of pre-war farms."

As Congressman Fjare of the committee said musingly, "if defense construction stopped immediately, Guam would be in a bad fix." The outbreak of peace in the world, for example, could be a catastrophe for the Guamanian people, as a result of the mold into which the U.S. has forced its life.

And the Guam Legislature has its hands tied as far as doing anything about it is concerned. Since 1941 Guam has been designated as an "A and C defense area," and any going in or out has to be cleared by the navy. This is still in effect, even for American citizens, including Guamanians.

This is a hardship and hinders us from developing the island, said Won Pat; "it is difficult for us to create some kind of economy other than the military because everything there is controlled largely by the military. We feel as leaders of the community that we must provide something for a cushion in case the military activities there fluctuate and we recognize that the economy of the island is superficial or artificial."

Now this cramping of the economy into a mold to suit a foreign occupation is one of the reasons why today the Philippines, although independent, has such economic difficulties. (The same has gone on in Puerto Rico under more than 50 years of American control.) The U.S. can get Filipinos as coolie laborers in Guam today for the same reason, in part, as leads the Guamanians to complain of the economic fate that threatens *them*.

One of the things that imperialist domination does — even the least brutal imperialism — is to prevent a people from developing in their own image, in accordance with their own needs, and in fulfillment of their own culture, economic paths and interests. Imperialism twists and distorts their life in every way.

That is shown in the comparatively small scale cases of Guam and Samoa as well as, or better than, in the bigger cases of India or Algeria.

Labor Action
December 24, 1956

Who Cares About Samoa?

The Pacific island group of American Samoa is by no means the most blatant example of colonialism; there are far worse cases, to put it mildly. But there is one thing about it which makes it important to Americans: the colonialist in this case is the United States government. And no one seems to care about what is going on there.

The U.S. has very few colonial areas over which it exercises direct political domination. That is not the characteristic form that American imperialism takes. The Philippines and Cuba\ even became white elephants and were turned loose. The main form of American imperialism is usually exercised through economic and indirect political domination and control — a quite different subject of inquiry. The few exceptions are retained by the U.S. not decisively for reasons of economic exploitation but mainly for military reasons — i.e., ancillary to the bigger problems of American imperialism in the world.

In addition to Okinawa (Ryukyus) and Puerto Rico, to both of which we have in the past devoted attention, there are also: the Panama Canal Zone; the Virgin Islands; American Samoa; Guam and the Marianas; the Trust Territory of the Pacific, which includes the Marshall Islands and others; and some scattered islands many of which have no native population, like Wake, Midway, etc. (Hawaii and Alaska are different cases.)

The fact that the decisive reason for holding on to these possessions is not economic underlines the meaning of what has been taking place there; for there is nothing that inherently *drives* the U.S. to exploit their peoples, as France is driven to exploit Algeria. In fact, in many cases Washington would like to be a quite benevolent master — provided that benevolence doesn't cost too much, doesn't get in anybody's way, doesn't annoy the military, doesn't "cause any trouble" — in fact, provided so many things that the best way the native peoples can avoid being a "nuisance" is to take whatever is done to them and not complain.

But that doesn't happen. They complain. But to whom can they complain? Who is willing to listen?

In the course of 1956 a disgraceful operation has taken place with respect to Samoa and Guam. It was all public. Yet there has hardly been a peep about it in the United States. After it was all over, there was a letter in the N. Y. *Times* correspondence column — that's about all.

Congress had passed a law suspending the application of U.S. minimum wage standards to Samoa; at the last minute Guam was not included in this suspension, but as we shall see in another study, that makes no difference.

To learn what was behind this, one has to go to the two volumes of testimony that came out of the hearings on this law before a House subcommittee during February to April of the past year.

In brief, we learn that for several years, with full knowledge of what was going on, the government has deliberately been permitting the complete ignoring of U.S. labor standards in the exploitation of native labor under the American flag.

There is a real coolie labor system not only flourishing under the American flag but *encouraged* by the government!

The issue became sharp when it was discovered several years ago, to Washington's dismay, that the U.S. minimum wage law actually applied not only to the 48 states but also to possessions overseas.

This discovery was very disconcerting, because the law was not being enforced. Not only that: *the government had not, and has not, the slightest intention of ever enforcing it.*

People who have a mechanical notion of capitalist legality may think this incredible. It happens to be a public fact. And it has been going on for years, and is still going on.

The United States government is openly, publicly and admittedly breaking the law, in order not to interfere with the coolie wage system which would be blown up if the law were ever enforced.

This went on with no difficulty as long as it was merely up to the executive arm of the government. There would be a difficulty, very likely, however, if the issue ever came before the courts, which are inclined to be less accommodating. For example, suppose someone brought suit to collect what was due to the defrauded workers . . . ? A suit could be brought not only for the wages not being paid now, but also to collect for *back* wages that should have been paid going all the way back to the Brown-Vermilya decision, or perhaps to the very passage of the minimum wage law. . . .

So this past year bills were drawn and presented in Congress to do two things: (1) kill the application of the minimum wage law in the possessions, particularly Guam and Samoa; (2) exempt the affected employers *retroactively* from their liability for the back wages that they should have been paying.

The first objective was formulated in the bills as a measure to amend the minimum wage law in these places. (It is this change that has already been passed for Samoa.)

One by-product of this mess is that a spotlight was cast on the conditions in these Pacific islands leading up to the situation. For the first time some information came out, when a subcommittee of the House committee on Education and Labor held a series of hearings on the bills, beginning February 15 and ending April 18, 1956.

At these hearings, the AFL-CIO's legislative representative Walter J. Mason quite rightly stressed that "there is an almost total vacuum of down-to-earth reliable factual information about the Samoan economy, the level of wages in Samoa" and many other things, and this is true also of the social and political conditions of the islanders' lives. Anyone can verify the existence of this almost total vacuum by looking up Samoa in New York's best reference library. Nobody seems to care.

But now the two volumes of the congressional hearings themselves constitute an exception. Let's see what they reveal.

American Samoa is the name given to the eastern group of the Samoan Islands; Western samoa is presently under the New Zealand flag. The history of the imperialist scramble in the Pacific for possession of these lands is a very edifying one, but we skip it at this time.

Suffice to say that in 1878 the U.S. got itself a coaling station for ships at Pago; in 1899 the islands were partitioned between the U.S. and Germany; the U.S. was interested in the Pago Pago harbor and therefore the administration of the islands was turned over to the navy. Although official commissions looked in and reported and plans were drawn, Congress never enacted any legislation setting up a permanent government for Samoa.

After the Second World War, it ceased to be of naval importance and is now not regarded as needed for a base. So in July 1951 the administration was taken over by the Interior Department.

Samoans are *not* citizens; their status is that of American "nationals" only. The governor, appointed by the Interior Department, is a dictator pure-and-simple. There is a native legislature with advisory status called the *Fono*, but the governor is the law. He is also the president of the island's bank and the editor of the island's newspaper — Lord Poo-bah himself.

For example, at the hearings Mason was asked whether the AFL-CIO has any unions in Samoa; the question was designed to intimate that he had no interest to represent in the matter and was only wasting the committee's time. Mason riposted smartly:

No . . . I don't know whether we would be allowed to go there and organize them. Samoa does not have an organic act. The governor is the law. He makes the laws. We do not have a government by law in

105

Samoa; we have a government by men. We think this matter should be the first consideration of this Congress in trying to help to build up the economy of Samoa.

If you have read Margaret Mead's popular *Coming of Age in Samoa,* an anthropologist's study of the native culture, you have some idea of the cultural background of the people. But this study was made in the 1920s in outlying islands, and does not offer a guide to conditions in present day Tutuila.

One background historical fact is indispensable. The Samoans have not been very docile colonial subjects.

Even before World War I, Western Samoa developed a native dissident movement — *Mau* (Opinion) movement — which caused the then German masters a good deal of trouble. After that war, under the New Zealand mandate, disaffection increased and the Mau movement was revived, with the slogan "Samoa for the Samoans," national symbols and a separate native government. There was stubborn fighting; a native boycott of things European; a disobedience campaign and an antitax payment movement — all for the demand of autonomy and the end of European control and exploitation. Later, under a Labor government, New Zealand made peace with the Mau movement through concessions.

The Mau movement also appeared in American Samoa, under navy rule. Concessions in form were made, including the setting up of the advisory Fono. It is not for nothing that the Samoans have been called "the Irishmen of the Pacific" — i.e., scrappy troublemakers from the point of view of the imperialists.

The current problem in Samoa concerns its economy. It is an intriguing and perhaps a unique case. Everybody has heard of one-industry economies in underdeveloped areas. Samoa is not merely a one-industry economy. It is a one-plant economy.

That is, while there is the native agriculture which provides the sustenance for the majority of the people, the industrial economy of the island consists of one solitary plant in Pago Pago, a tunafish cannery of the Van Camp company, whose main plants are in California.

We have here in some respects a laboratory specimen, isolated for easy inquiry, of some typical problems, including the rationalizations used for the exploitation of, native labor.

There had been a previous attempt to establish a fishing and cannery industry in Pago Pago, but it did not pan out. the land and buildings, owned by the government, were leased to Van Camp. The following information was contributed by the Van Camp man, William Moore, who testified at the congressional hearings:

Van Camp began by using the cannery equipment, land and buildings owned by the government, though it also had to add to the equipment. For a 5-year lease, it paid a rent in the neighborhood of only $2500 a year.

The company pays no taxes on the plant.

The 300 cannery workers (Samoans) are mostly women. Moore endorsed their energy and aptitude, so he was not complaining about the quality of labor, though of course skill had to be built up.

These workers are not covered by social security, nor by unemployment compensation, nor by several other U.S. labor laws, like the antikickback act or the Walsh-Healey Act.

Their wage rates start from 27 cents an hour, the average about 40 cents. And because of layoffs and seasonal work, a worker's total income for the year is about $450.

This coolie wage scale is in a *high price* economy, comparable to the U.S.'s price scale.

In spite of these sweatshop conditions, Moore complained that the company had lost money in its first year of operation — $200,000, a drop in the bucket. But under questioning, he admitted that "some part" of the loss (how much he didn't know or wouldn't say) was simply due to the capital investment that had to be put in, especially an expensive refrigerator plant. At the end of the second year, the loss was down to $30,000 and even Moore was hopeful of getting into profitable black. The further mounting of the profit-take would depend, however, on the continuation of the coolie system.

But, like the congressional committee, Moore frankly and fully realized that there was a slight difficulty: *all this was completely illegal!* That in itself would not bother them; but as we explained, what if some troublemaker should sue?

James Roosevelt (D.-Cal.), a member of the subcommittee, for whom Van Camp is a respected constituent, was worried about this situation: "it is something that might become very, very serious to them because there is back pay for over 300 people piling up there," he remarked at one point.

And later: it's a risk, he said, because "if an American national could sue, there is always a possibility that some bright lawyer would go down there and file a suit. . . ." An appalling thought, especially since not a single gentleman in the hearing room had any doubt that the law was being violated.

The record shows that not for a split second did any of them raise any question of getting the workers their due. They were trying to figure out how to quash any liability action. Not for a second did any government representative or congressman ever suggest that the law should be enforced!

The Roosevelt scion had other constituents in California too, and he had to cover himself. At one time he raised the question in effect: Aren't these Samoan cannery workers taking the bread out of the mouth of our California workers? How much of Van Camp's work is shifting to Samoa? "I would want to be awfully sure I was not building up here [Samoa] a low-wage scale competitive operation which in time would ruin the position of the American worker on the West Coast. . . ." But vaguely assured by Moore that it was only a small percentage of Van Camp's operation, he dropped the subject.

Later, however, the committee got a protest from the Seafarers International Union in San Francisco. The union pointed out that Van Camp workers in California get a minimum hourly wage of $1.65 (women) and $1.85 (men); the Samoan plant is unfair competition because of the low-wage conditions; other canners would be moved to take advantage of coolie labor in the South Sea island territories; and "the U.S. Congress cannot treat these people as fourth-class citizens."

It is not only a matter of competition for stateside plants. It is also a question of establishing privileged sanctuaries for runaway sweatshops, worse perhaps than the role being played nowadays by the South or by Puerto Rico.

For example, the government has had another proposal for the establishment of a plant in Samoa: from the Exquisite Brassiere Company, which is now operating in Puerto Rico as well as in the states. If the Van Camp experiment is financially successful, then the white man's civilization may register the cultural triumph of putting Samoan women and brassieres into the same picture.

But, complained the Interior Department, the brassiere sweat shop won't come in as long as the minimum wage provision hangs over its head. A procession of government representatives (Interior, Labor, State, Defense) came before the committee to warn that paying the U.S. wage "would upset the economic balance" in Samoa.

Well, *why* do they claim that paying U.S. wages would be so fatal to the Samoan economy? What would be so terrible about giving the people more money? Throughout the hearings, the government spokesmen reply "It is obvious . . ." or "It goes without saying . . ." or "There is no doubt, of course . . ." that paying decent wages would do appalling things to the people, but not one finds it possible to explain.

For example, Interior Department rep Arnold told the committee:

It will readily be seen, we are sure, that any application of stateside wage scales to industrial activity in American Samoa would completely disrupt the local economy, impose price inflation upon the people and create serious personnel and financial problems for the territorial government, to say nothing of the impact which such a situation would exert on the prevailing economic conditions of neighboring islands and territories.

But this "local economy" which would be "disrupted" — remember — consists of *one* plant. There is no economic mystery about the meaning of the doubletalk.

Governor Lowe, before the committee, also said that "It is evident" that "the American standard of wages" would disrupt the "entire local economy." It is one case where a governor not only can be personally acquainted with "the entire local economy" but even invite him over for dinner.

The governor also explained:

The main commodity which is readily available is that of labor in an area which is surrounded by the territories of other nations, all of whom have pay standards well below the minimums in the U.S. . . . Some day the Territory may be ready for the minimum wages applicable within the U.S. but when that day will be is anybody's guess. Certainly it is not today.

Is the idea, then, that Samoa must wait until the surrounding territories get a comparable wage? Will New Zealand (which runs Western Samoa) have trouble keeping the people in line with a pittance if American Samoans get a decent wage? This is, indeed, part of the government position.

In other words, the terrible things that would happen if the minimum wage law were enforced would be terrible for sweatshop employers not only in the territory but also in the region; but not for the people who are supposed to be Washington's wards. It is no wonder that the Samoans themselves are not impressed by the arguments about the "disruption" of their economy.

The U.S. has run into this same problem in many other places — for example, Morocco, where the French rulers used to get apoplexy at the idea of permitting high U.S. wages to "spoil" the natives. As long as Morocco was under the French, the U.S. went along with the local imperialist exploiters, as elsewhere.

Congressman Aspinall lifted a veil on another point:

For decades the Navy controlled the islands ... They paid higher wages. And during that time, of course, the economy of the islands was kind of puffed up. Then they went out, and civilian control came in, and we have had trouble ever since then as far as maintaining the right kind of a level in their economy is concerned.

This congressman also made a strange point: "if a small segment of the population [the cannery workers] were the only part that were able to get these desired luxuries . . . the rest of them would be, of course, discontented all the time." Mr. Aspinall seems to be for an equalitarian society in Samoa, so long as it an equality of poverty.

But the bluntest statement came from Professor Felix Keesing, a thorough imperialist who has also acted as a publicist for the navy. His letter to the committee was put into the record. It is clear what he is afraid of:

[The minimum wage] would have unfortunate repercussions upon these other territories [of other powers in the South Pacific] and so upon our national friends and allies. It would tend to breed discontent among the peoples in these neighboring islands and complicate problems of trusteeship and welfare. . . .

The wage scale issue is part of a larger political problem, that of relations between Samoan leaders and the U.S. executive and Congress. . . . Persons familiar with the South Pacific know that Samoa has a long history of disturbance which can still rise to the surface when the Samoan stake appears to the people to be threatened. Introduction of the mainland wage scale, putting much larger amounts of money especially into the hands of younger individuals, could be a sudden undermining force to the Samoan economic and social system, and so endanger what otherwise would be an orderly longer-term adjustment to the Western way of life. This would likewise have political repercussions. Political disturbances in such an overseas territory reflect on the good name of the U.S. and open the way to deleterious international criticisms of American administrative policies.

So it is fairly clear that the terrible "danger" to be avoided is not any danger *to the Samoan people;* rather, it seems to be a danger *from* the Samoan people.

All of this is based on an assumption: that the speedy industrialization of Samoa is not only a good thing in and of itself but indeed practically vital for the interests of the people, their only practical economic path of progress right here and now.

Is that so? We may tend to take it for granted because we know it is so in many other underdeveloped areas. But the question has to be raised not only on an economic level but also on a cultural one: the impact of one culture on another and its responsibilities.

The only one who showed any consciousness that such a problem exists was the representative of the AFL-CIO, Mason. "I am not too sure," he said, "with the established customs that they have, that they want an industry of this kind. . . ." He made a counter suggestion: the Samoans already have a native handicraft industry, poorly developed because it is hard to organize export of the products, since few ships stop at the island; why not start with what they have, and help? . . .

The AFL-CIO man, by the way, was not only the only one at the hearings to suggest the cultural problem but also the only one who defended the interests of the Samoans themselves. I find this an illuminating case: Mason was no anti-imperialist radical but a conservative trade unionist; yet the material interest of labor in the situation drove him to approach the issue from the broadest social viewpoint, and progressively. Only labor did this, no one else; because of its basic social situation, and despite the immaturity of its political ideas.

Correction: There was one other, apparently brought down by Mason — a *Samoan* spokesman, Vaiinupo J. Ala'ilima, a young man residing in this country. For the first time the committee heard the viewpoint of the Samoans themselves.

Ala'ilima presented a sort of credential, a letter from his kinsman, the high chief Palepoi (whose grandfather had ceded the island to the U.S. in 1900). It referred to "those wicked officials who are here" and who should leave Samoa, and asked Ala'ilima to "present my case and promote my interest . .

. and the interest of your country. . . . Things are in tragic condition at present.
. . ."

Ala'ilima, 29, explained that he had been reared in American Samoa "inside
the naval station" since he was 6; worked there during and after the war; had
been among the first graduates of the new high school. He had left in 1950,
among those who had gone to the U.S. "for the purpose of learning so that we
may return home and help our people." In this country he had studied law and
civil engineering at a couple of Midwest colleges; at present he was working
for the U.S. Engineering Corps, Design Branch, as an engineering aide.

His testimony was that of a highly intelligent, sensitive, and informed
person, far superior in every respect to the Southern congressman with whom
the committee is loaded, who so obviously patronized him. He began with a
tribute to the AFL-CIO's position in the hearing. "It certainly is encouraging
to learn that we have a wise and true friend among your people," he said.

Then he read a paper which brilliantly summarized the case for the
Samoans' right to the U.S. minimum dollar wage.

(1) "To help our economy": At present the people getting the substandard
wage in Samoa "can hardly provide for food, clothing and shelter for
themselves and their families." Unskilled laborers are even worse off. When
he was working there, he recounted, "I was only able to buy food and have a
little money to give for my religious contribution. I was not able to provide
shelter and clothing for myself." Now the cost of living is much higher "and
therefore conditions are much worse for the wage earner."

He explained the family-communal basis of Samoan life: "our economy is
based on sharing." If one worker makes the dollar wage, then his family back
on the soil will also benefit; all of Samoan society would progress.

"This is promoting and stabilizing our economy, not wrecking it as the
Department of the Interior, our governor and others lead you to believe."

(2) The minimum wage will "protect our people from being exploited for
cheap labor" and will enable us to bring in industrialization slowly and
gradually. It was an unhealthy situation during the war when most of our
people were wage earners. Exempting Samoa from the wage act "in order to
attract industries to come down and ruin us is just like asking a respectable
citizen to open his house to attract profiteers. . . . What are we going to offer
you? A few pennies and a polluted area, individualism and money madness,
poor health and constant worries?. . ."

If the Fono had gone along with the government position, he said, it was
because they didn't know better. It is false to claim that the people's "social

structure" will be disrupted. "The only social structure and economic conditions that will be upset will be those of the governor and his administration officials, the Van Camp stateside employees and other industries. They will be required to pay more money for their domestic employees.

(3) "It is not fair for unskilled laborers of other territories and possessions to receive better wages than we do when our cost of living is comparably high or even higher."

As for the argument about the effect on neighboring territories run by other powers, he made a shrewd hit: Why doesn't the U.S. worry about that with regard to the neighboring nations with whom *you* do business and which are directly affected by *your* industries and labor conditions?

He proceeded to show that the Samoan workers of Van Camp have been setting a high standard of productiveness, far beyond their low wages. Also: the stateside people brought in to supervise are less skilled, yet they get infinitely more: "I suppose they feel that the justice and greatness of this nation and democracy is best portrayed by such unjust actions," he added bitingly.

He did not omit a direct assault on Governor Lowe as a dictator with no qualifications whatsoever for the task of governing the Samoan people.

More than once he emphasized that higher wages on the island would mean that the people could afford better education, and thus improve their lot. (The education system provided by the government is pretty miserable, by the way, as shown in other sections of the government hearing. For example, after the 9th grade, only selected children can go to high school, only 70 out of about 200 applicants. Some of the school children go all day without any lunch, and none is provided. Most of the high school teachers are wives of other government employees; that saves the cost of bringing over real teachers. Scholarships are nonexistent or meager.)

Ala'ilima, it should be noted, did not come out against industrialization; not at all. He was against a quickie and indiscriminate industrialization at the expense of the people's economic conditions and cultural integrity. ("And the culture that we have, the real Samoan culture that we have, many parts of it have been ruined by the coming of the navy, the kind of government that the navy sent to us.")

What he wanted was a gradual industrialization. The committee chairman asked him challengingly: Would you prefer that Van Camp leave the island rather than stay there and pay substandard wages? He answered, "I believe so," and he tried to explain how the economy imported by the navy, in it day, had injured the society.

The people had become dependent on the foreigners. "And they didn't stress much the program whereby we can develop our land to its utmost." They didn't want to educate and lift up the people; they wanted only natives who could understand some minimum things.

The concept he was getting at was this: the white men had come in and, while destroying the old proud independent Samoan, had not replaced him with a new Samoan trained in new civilized ways, but rather with — native coolies whom they could exploit. The best of the old culture was being undermined and the best of the new culture was not being made available.

Ala'ilima's own program for Samoan development was to start with development of agriculture: "the future of our country lies in the land." Let Samoa first develop an agriculture on modern lines, that could really support the island, before it becomes all-dependent on industries that can exploit the people for low wages.

If agriculture were in a healthy state, then the people could resist exploitation when industry came in; it would have to come in on the people's terms, not taking advantage of dire need. "That is not what we need. What we need at present — the almighty dollar will ruin us if it is just for the sake of almighty dollars."

In short: develop agriculture first; then gradually bring in industries "that will meet our conditions and our resources at home."

Whether Ala'ilima's program is the best way is something we certainly can't say; we do not claim to be a Samoan expert. But this is absolutely and unqualifiedly certain from a reading of the record. Not a single one of the government representatives, not a single one of the committee congressmen, not a single one of the stateside representatives who testified, ever entertained a second's thought on how to develop Samoa for the benefit of the Samoans.

Now that the navy no longer needs Samoa for its purposes, and since the island is in any case no rich plum for exploitation, it is today mainly a nuisance for the U.S. government. Its usefulness has been squeezed, and now let's not be bothered. Its culture has been ruined, but let Van Camp and its sweatshop wages fill the vacuum.

Civilize 'em at 27 cents an hour. Let the Exquisite Brassiere Company bear the White Man's Burden. And above all, they better not make any trouble. What's the matter, they think we owe them something maybe?

Labor Action
December 17, 1956

Kennedy's Disastrous Cuban Policy

Introductory Note

This article was part of a symposium, published soon after the events, in the Fall 1962 issue of New Politics. *The symposium comprised four pieces from (the editor said) different points of view, followed by five articles about Castro's Cuba in general. The four writers who allegedly represented a spectrum of viewpoints on the missile crisis were, besides me, Norman Thomas, Victor Alba, and Professor Robert J. Alexander. Not one of these criticized President Kennedy for threatening to throw the world into a nuclear war if America's overlordship were not respected by Khrushchev.*

This was part of the immediate context for the article, since in it I hoped to speak to far different sorts of leftists than those who could read Alba and Alexander without losing their breakfast. In a broader sense, I was especially exercised over the idea in the first sentence of my article. I still am. It remains a fact, to this day, that only an American president has put his finger on the Red Button, and threatened to blow up the world, that is, start World War Three, unless the enemy gave in to his demands. Neither then nor later has anyone ever answered the question: why is it so impermissible for the Russians to hold a base ninety miles off our shores, while we can ring their frontiers with military bases — so impermissible that the only punishment that fits the crime is the launching of World War Three? For me this was not primarily a question of morality but of an issue which will comprise a separate number in this series, on Political Warfare.

H. D.

The long and short of U.S. policy in the last Cuba crisis was that Kennedy threatened to engulf the world in a nuclear war unless Moscow capitulated to his demands.

We won. We showed 'em. They can't push us around. Kennedy was right all the time. Just meet 'em with force and they'll back down. That's the language they understand. This was the triumphant talk that arose, after a sigh of relief, when Khrushchev agreed to dismantle the bases and the world receded from the brink. This reaction is the most dangerous thing that has happened in American public opinion since the beginning of the Cold War. Not only is it basically false, as we shall see, but it means that, the next time, there will be so much less resistance in the United States to an aggressive, adventuristic military-based foreign policy in reaction to Cold War crises.

Those who reacted with this kind of triumphant talk are, in the last analysis, sure of only one thing: that bringing the world to the brink of war was better than appeasement of the Kremlin; that "better dead than red" is better said than "better red than dead." It is only insofar as they choose between these alternatives that they manage to work up any confidence in their policy. But for the next time, or for some next time after that, there had better be a third way, or else this world is through.

It is most particularly "the next time" that I am interested in here: that is, the implications of this crisis for the future. For I am going to suggest, among other things, that a greater shift has taken place in Washington than the celebrants seem to realize. Just before Kennedy announced his blockade, Joseph Alsop wrote in his column: "Complicating the dreadfully dangerous Berlin problem by a harebrained, immediate attack on the Cuban problem would be an action so irresponsible that it deserves to be called criminal." Alsop had, earlier this year, had a sufficiently cast iron stomach to report in a *Saturday Evening Post* interview that Kennedy contemplated the possibility of the U.S.'s using nuclear weapons first; this he had *not* been moved to call criminal. It is not often that such a very reasonable person denounces the government's act as a crime, even in advance. It should make one wonder even in the midst of rejoicing.

I offer five propositions on the Cuba crisis.

The First Proposition is that this is *not* the issue as far as U.S. policy is concerned.

Of course, anyone who thinks that Castro is the paladin of revolutionary progress and liberty in Cuba has a simple job in choosing sides. It is not that simple for me. I am not an admirer of or political supporter of either Castro or his regime; I believe he is leading the Cuban revolution into the ditch; I believe he is an increasingly authoritarian dictator, and that as long as this is true he is ruining the Cuban revolution — whether he breaks with the Communists tomorrow or not. (The purely Stalinophobe basis of anti-Castroism is liable to get a little shaky.) Not the least of Castro's sins had been his willingness to make Cuba a pawn in the Cold War between the rival imperialist war camps.

In fact, on the Cold War level, the whole debate that took place in the UN reeked of the Pot and the Kettle. As I. F. Stone rightly put it in visceral terms, "The speeches of both Stevenson and Zorin to the Security Council Tuesday night [October 23] were equally nauseating." Adlai Stevenson, a broken man convicted last year of lying before the whole world, trumpeted about the "world civil war . . . between the pluralistic world and the monolithic world," but his pluralistic world put the gun to the heads of the Latin American states and came up with a monolithic vote of the Organization of American States. The Russian liar, on the other hand, spoke of the principle of noninterference in the internal affairs of other states — such as Hungary, no doubt. Whatever Khrushchev's calculation may have been, exactly, in planting missile bases on Cuba in this situation, his motivation certainly was neither to defend Cuba nor ease war tensions.

But there is a great gulf between rejecting Castro's leadership of the Cuban revolution and supporting Washington's onslaughts on Cuba. One did not have to be a supporter of Nasser to condemn the British-French-Israeli imperialist aggression on Suez in 1956. One did not even have to be a supporter of Imre Nagy to condemn the Russian suppression of Hungary, and many a Communist Party was ripped open because there were Communists who saw this point. It is true that much of the exposé literature about the bureaucratization of the Castro regime is used for — and some of it was written to be used for — the whitewashing of Washington's squeeze on Cuba, just as Arthur Schlesinger, Jr. lamented Castro's "betrayal" of the Cuban revolution for the sake of whitepapering the CIA mounted invasion at the Bay of Pigs. But this use of scholars does not make the truth about Castro less true; it merely makes it necessary to face also the truth about Kennedy. Castro's antidemocracy motivates nothing whatsoever in the Cuba policy of a United States which mobilizes a Somoza and an Ydigoras to denounce this antidemocracy.

Nor, remember, was it those missile bases which steeled Kennedy's heart against Cuba, although we must assume they precipitated the last crisis.* A year ago there were no missile bases in Cuba, and no jet bombers; indeed, émigré gunboats could shoot up Cuban harbors with impunity. But the U.S. invaded. After the fiasco, Kennedy's speech to the editors' convention virtually threatened that he was not giving up the idea: "Our patience is not endless," he intoned. It had nothing to do with missile bases or offensive

---

* In my opinion, an examination of the evidence - especially the chronology - strongly supports the view that Kennedy's move was at least *triggered off* by the exigencies of the election campaign; I am not discussing this factor here simply to save space.

threats then, did it? A half-decent memory makes it difficult to swallow the story that that is all Kennedy is mad about.

Subversive thoughts like these are held even by Kennedy's best friends. The New York *Times* of October 23, 1963, stated that his British supporters defended action against Cuba because Castro's regime "would accelerate a general swing to the left in Latin America."

On that same October 23rd, I found myself at the University of Chicago, one of whose luminaries is Prof. Hans Morgenthau, an ardent supporter of the blockade, whose only complaint was that Kennedy had not done something sooner. In the University paper one could read:

> Morgenthau stated that the threat posed by the presence of missiles in Cuba "does not add materially to the direct military threat already present".

> The significance of the presence of missiles is twofold, stated Morgenthau. First, it is a threat to U.S. prestige. Second, it creates an effective showplace of modern weapons to show other Latin American countries, and in this way could aid in the training of subversives in Latin America. [Chicago *Maroon*, October 24.]

This is a more cynical view of what was involved, but, I think, a more candid one. For Moscow, too, the Nagy regime in Hungary would have been a danger not because it was run by "fascists" or by the CIA, but because its very existence would accelerate the desire to go-and-do-likewise in East Europe, because it was blow to the Kremlin's prestige, and because it was a kind of showplace.

Kennedy's entire case for the blockade was based on the distinction between "offensive weapons" and "defensive weapons." This distinction was made something fundamental and absolute. Without it, there would not be a shred left to the U.S. position even formally. Considering the almost total lack of any defense of this theory, one would think it was well established and respectable. Yet the fact is that every informed person knows it is a fraud.

I know of three attempts to discuss this theory, though no doubt there were more. The New York *Times'* military expert Hanson Baldwin remarked (the day after Kennedy made his announcement) that "the manner in which a weapon is used rather than the weapon itself is the best yardstick for classification" as defensive or offensive. He added that "the MIG jet fighters [not bombers] now in Cuban hands emphasize even more that missiles the danger of classifying any weapon as 'defensive' or 'offensive'. . . . All of these types are useful as fighter interceptors. But all can easily fly over Florida and other parts of the southeastern U.S., and like our own fighter interceptors many of them could be armed with various types of conventional or nuclear arms, including rockets and bombs."

David Lawrence's Washington column on October 24 said:

For several months the American government has known that missile bases were being built and equipped in Cuba. But, up to now, the official assumption has been that all this was "defensive" on Cuba's part. There is, however, little difference actually between a missile base built for defense and one built for offensive purposes.

He made no effort to relate this interesting observation to the cheers for Kennedy in the rest of his column.

The Irish delegate to the UN discussed this in his speech of October 24. Here is his attempt:

There is some force to the argument often used that whether a weapon is to be regarded as offensive or defensive depends less on its intrinsic character than on the intentions of those who posses it. Whatever may be the intentions of the Soviet or Cuban government, however, it appears undeniable that the installations, missiles and aircraft now in Cuba are capable, in the hands of ill-intentioned persons, of constituting a deadly threat to the security of North and South America.

Or, to put the same thought in other words, the distinction is absurd. The criterion has become *political* — the evil intentions in the mind of the other fellow. It will be time to discuss this seriously when the UN, or even the U.S., dreams of applying this distinction to any other country.

But why is it necessary to quote authority on this? There is a more decisive question which has only to be asked to explode this fraudulent position: *Are the United States' military preparations offensive or defensive?* Take its ICBMS (on which it has specialized whereas Russia has concentrated on smaller- range missiles), its Polaris submarines, its strategic bombers, its overseas bases on Russia's border — *are these offensive or defensive weapons?*

Or is it only and exclusively in the case of a tiny country threatened by a giant that weapons automatically become offensive if they are capable, of striking outside its own borders?

Kennedy insists that jet bombers too are often "offensive weapons" and must be removed from Cuba. Is there any other country in the world that would allow itself to be stripped in this way on the claim that it is automatically an offensive threat against its neighbors? While the U.S. itself has been arming the Latin American caudillos, has it been supplying their armies only with "defensive weapons?" Let us have an accounting.

I have not, myself, seen a single honest admission from supporters of the blockade that what Castro, with Russian aid, was resorting to, in the face of the real threat of invasion by the U.S., was the famous policy of the deterrent — nothing more!

Now, I am against deterrent politics as it is practiced in this Cold War; but I am not against it only when it is practiced by Cuba to deter the United States. The supporters of Kennedy, however, are for it. It is the very heart of U.S. foreign policy today. They extol it as the only way to keep in check a would be aggressor. Anyone who is dubious about it as the last word in international wisdom is denounced or derided. Shall the Cubans remain unconvinced by all this?

It is a hundred times true that for Moscow to build up Cuba as a nuclear missile base is provocative, but *it is only left critics of U.S. policy who have the moral right to denounce either Khrushchev or Castro for this.* In supporters of the Kennedy policy which produced the blockade, such denunciation is a kind of naive hypocrisy which has become so built in to current American thinking that it can even be done by honest men.

The glee over the Famous Victory is a little premature. One can easily understand the outburst: in the first place, there was an election won; in the second place, Americans have not had much to crow about in a long time. It tickled every *Daughter of the American Revolution's* patriotic heart to see us upstanding Americans ordering Russian ships around.

But who really won what? This is still to be seen: who will reap the greatest gain from this episode.

The dominant American reaction is clearly a sick one. It has the function of relieving the doomful sense of frustration that hangs over America's role in the Cold War.

What is emphasized almost exclusively in the American celebration over the blockade is Khrushchev's "loss of face": he backed down; he capitulated; we were top dog; our "nerve did not flinch" (Lord Home). The image, of course, is exactly the same as that of juvenile predelinquents playing the game of Chicken. The press writes almost as a matter of course that Russia lost influence in the world because it backed down when Kennedy rose in all his wrath and brandished his thunderbolts.

Russia lost influence with whom?

The press tells of reactions in foreign capitals, by political spokesmen, etc. We have still to find out whether the Kremlin lost influence with plain people when it declined to meet Kennedy's war challenge.

Does anyone think it was only Bertrand Russell who reacted by hailing Khrushchev as the preserver of peace? Now, no one need work hard to prove to me that Russell is not a political genius, but derogatory remarks about his political capacity are beside the point. Brazilian peasants or Italian workers or Indonesian officers are also not as politically sophisticated as the types who write apologias for the State Department.

What has Khrushchev really lost? (Besides "face," that is.) Did he lose Cuba? Leaving aside the questions of whether he "had" Cuba, what exactly does Russia need a Cuban satellite for? I am not sure that anyone pays much attention to the official theory that Moscow has or had any permanent perspective for Cuba as a serious military base. And a Cuban satellite will certainly not be an economic asset to the Russian empire.

The basic use that Khrushchev has for Cuba is as a *political* pawn, as a battering ram in *political warfare* against the United States. And when the instrument is used up in his hands and has to be tossed away, this is an old story for the Kremlin totalitarians. That's Castro' neck, not theirs.

The question then is this: Which will attract the people of the world: the image of Kennedy as Mars hurling Jovian thunderbolts, or of Khrushchev as the Jovial Peacelover?

But this is only the immediate side of things. Having established himself as a Peacelover, Khrushchev still has to make his next move.

Will it be a squeeze on the U.S.'s Turkish bases? Kennedy has put into Khrushchev's bank a small fortune in political capital. Khrushchev has only to decide how to spend it. It is the simplest thing in the world to write an editorial in an *American* newspaper explaining why the U.S. cannot tolerate Cuba but Moscow must tolerate U.S. nuclear bases on its own border: all you have to do is ignore elementary logic and common sense and not many will notice the difference. It is a little harder to explain it to anyone else in the world, which is filled with deplorably un-American types. I have a substantial and entertaining collection of clippings bearing elucidations by certified thinkers on the basic difference between Cuban and Turkish bases, but the varieties are few.

The very first was Kennedy's own, when he said in his blockade announcement: "Our own strategic weapons have never been transferred to another nation *under the cloak of secrecy.*" (Emphasis added.) Unfortunately, Kennedy did not mean that the Russians' move would have been all right if done openly, so this masterpiece of smugness does not help much.*

It has been asked: Wouldn't it be considered provocative if the U.S. were to establish *new* military bases in, say, Finland? To be sure, I would so consider it, myself, but this is of no consequence: would the supporters of Kennedy's current Realpolitik denounce it? It is very easy to claim this when there is, in fact, little possibility of eventuation; but the U.S. bases in Korea, Japan, Taiwan, the Philippines, Turkey, Libya, Morocco, Italy, Spain, France, England, Germany, Holland, Iceland and Greenland were all once new, each in their turn. We did not hear them denounced as provocations by the people now defending the Kennedy blockade, as each of them in turn changed the then existing status quo. It is much easier to reject bases that do not exist.

More and more, however, formulations on the "basic difference" between the Cuban and Turkish bases come down to the rationale enunciated in the *Wall Street Journal*'s editorial effort on the subject (October 26): our bases are there to defend the "free world," theirs are there to destroy the said free world.

The whole point is that the U.S. *has to demonstrate* to a somewhat skeptical world that all it is doing is defending the "free world," and it cannot prove this by assuming it.

This is an argument which can literally justify anything, *and is so used*. When Russia crushed Hungary, this proved it was Bad. But when we invade Cuba, this is justified because we are Good. If Russia starts a nuclear war, this will be an historic war crime against humanity, of which only barbaric totalitarians

---

* This also raises a question pointed up only (as far as I have seen) by the best reporter in Washington, I. F. Stone, in his *Weekly*: Why did the Russians make not the slightest attempt to camouflage the missile bases? I have not seen any explanations of this by any government spokesman or apologist. The reasons that occur to one are all entirely incompatiblbbe with the government's official case.

are capable. But if the U.S. starts a nuclear war (as Kennedy says we may), then this will be to save the free world, because we are Good.

Let this smug, Pecksniffian doctrine really permeate the U.S. and those fingers in Washington will be twice as itchy to press the button. This is one of the most frightening developments of all — this blind, stupid self-righteousness oblivious to political reality.*

The other political bank in which Kennedy has deposited capital for Khrushchev is — the Berlin issue. Berlin is not 90 miles off the coast of the Communist world but right in the middle of its territory. There is conjecture about a possible new blockade of Berlin if the Russians want to get tough again. The last time, the blockade was beaten by an airlift. But surely the thought has occurred to our planners in Washington:

Now that Kennedy has told the world he was ready to sink Russian ships on the high seas in order to isolate an enemy base outside the U.S., what happens if Khrushchev announces (in a TV broadcast) that the East Germans will shoot down any American plane flying over their own territory against their wishes?

What do we do next to get tough: invade East Germany?

The degree to which the U.S. position is fantastically untenable has been nowhere more sharply pointed up than by Walter Lippman, in his column of October 23. The Turkish base, he argues is a liability now:

These things need to be understood by our people as we find ourselves in a military crisis over Cuba. Until our people do understand them, they will be thinking and feeling and voting in a world that no longer exists. In the world that now exists the United States is not omnipotent.

---

* Oblivious also to any question of legal rights of nations. Thus, Canada's Prime Minister Diefenbaker found himself telling his parliament that arguments about the legality of the blockade were "largely sterile and irrelevant." When Khrushchev talks like this about Western treaty rights to Berlin, these pious statesmen know hbbbbow to fulminate. Incidentally, Diefenbaker was backed up, of course, by opposition leader Pearson - a fact noteworthy only because the latter is a Nobel Peace Prize winner.

It cannot, therefore, enforce the Monroe Doctrine in the Western Hemisphere and the Truman Doctrine in the Eastern Hemisphere.

The appeasers, of course, will be happy to tell us that West Berlin must be surrendered to the Russians in order to keep them peaceful. But, precisely because we must reject such appeasement, Kennedy's Cuban policy is a first-class boon to Khrushchev's designs on Berlin, and above all to his ability to make political warfare out of the Berlin position. By backing down on Cuba, he has built up credit for himself. When and if he, in turn, gets tough on Berlin, the propaganda belts will whirr: "How can you accuse this eminent Peacelover of pushing war to the brink? Look how nice he was on Cuba — how understanding, how forbearing; how much he gave and gave. Now what is the U.S. going to do on this — not give an inch after all that? Do you want everything your own way? etc., etc.

It is not clear whether the Kennedy administration is shaping up a new foreign policy pattern or merely falling into it.

The New York *Times'* James Reston observes:

The new Kennedy style of diplomacy is now operating in the Cuban crisis. It is highly personal and national. It is power diplomacy in the old classic European sense that prevailed before the great men worried much about consulting with allies or parliaments or international organizations. [October 26]

"Power diplomacy in the old classic European sense" is what led to two world wars. But Kennedy is classic not only in the European sense. The classic formula of old fashioned American imperialism (the kind that used to send the marines into Nicaragua) was Theodore Roosevelt's "talk softly and carry a big stick." This is so notorious to students of history, like Kennedy, that it is positively startling to read that the President actually said in an October 13 election speech that "this is the time for a man who talks softly but who will also carry a big stick." Does he really think this is the time to go back to thinking in terms of charging up San Juan Hill?

The form in which Kennedy has rediscovered this vintage model of foreign policy is one of the simplest: hit first and let the other fellow decide what to do. Another of the Chicago professors of political science who gave

his thoughts on the subject saw no danger arising from the blockade for the
following reason:

> "Khrushchev may be a bold gambler, but he isn't crazy," stated [Prof.
> Morton] Kaplan. If we sink a ship, there isn't anything Russia can do,"
> he said.

If we sink a ship, there isn't anything Russia can do. I suggest that the reader turn
this over in his mind, savor to the full this proof that there is "no danger," in
order to enter the kind of thinking which Kennedy now represents. There isn't
anything Russia can do, our professor of political science means, except
retaliate with other steps that would lead right to nuclear war.

Now this works both ways. Let us suppose that the Communists shoot
down that plane over their territory going to Berlin; is there anything Kennedy
can do? except start the escalation to nuclear war?

If this sort of thing is so safe, then it is very tempting; and if it has led to
a Famous Victory once, why deprive ourselves of its beneficent effects? If we
move in and knock down that distasteful Berlin Wall, "there isn't anything
Russia can do." If the Russians move in and flatten that Turkish base, "there
isn't anything Kennedy can do." Or does it work on only one side?

Kennedy's admirers are applauding his new stance of "go-it-alone,"
especially on the right. (For example, William H. Chamberlin in the *Wall Street
Journal.*) This is the talk that was considered only a few short years ago to be
Hooverite neanderthalism. It was virtually the sole property of the horse-and-
buggy Republican Right, fought even by Eisenhower. Now it is the latest
model Stanley Steamer on the New Frontier.

That the new Kennedy stance *is* the hand-me-down of the Republican
Right was acted out in the election campaign. Who was yelling for this kind
of campaign when Kennedy turned around and gave it to them? If the tough
line on Cuba was such an effective antidote to the GOP's plan to make Cuba
the main election issue, it was so because Kennedy stole *their* line.

It has been said that Kennedy had to yield before right wing pressure. To
be sure, the right wing pressure was there. But Khrushchev also has a more
adventuristic and aggressive wing behind his back, it is said. So there is
justification for him to get tough too. . .

Where all this leads is right to the brink.

The N. Y. *Herald-Tribune* editorially chortled over exactly this the day after Kennedy's blockade announcement:

> . . . the moves already under way go to the brink of war. . . . One thing was remarkable about President Kennedy's response to the Soviet-Cuba threat. This was that he seemed to be going back to the Eisenhower administration's policy of "massive retaliation." . . . When the chips were down they went back to John Foster Dulles' theory of preventing war by threatening massive retaliation with nuclear weapons.

But while this eminent Republican organ is justified in claiming the copyright, there is still an important difference between the much maligned J. F. Dulles and the much hailed J.F. Kennedy; viz., Dulles invented the term and talked about it, but he never did it. *Kennedy is the first world leader to actually use the ultimatum of nuclear war as an instrument of national policy*, that is, to push the world to the literal brink of nuclear war. He is already sure of going down in history.

This question is formulated most often as a rhetorical justification for the President's action, as if the answer were self-evident. But there has been no crisis since the beginning of the Cold War where the alternatives were os plain and simple.

I leave aside here the alternative, suggested at the time all over the world, of taking the case to the United Nations instead of unilaterally threatening nuclear war, not because this is unimportant but because it is procedural in character. Let us discuss political alternatives.

Kennedy could have prevented any establishment of Russian missile bases in Cuba to begin with, without military re-course at all; or, failing that, definitively expose the Castro regime before its own friends and before all uncommitted forces.

The Cubans had made a solemn proposal before the United Nations in response to the Congressional Joint Resolution on Cuba: "Were the United States able to give Cuba effective guarantees and satisfactory proof concerning the integrity of Cuban territory, and were it to cease its subversive and counter-revolutionary activities against our people, then Cuba would not have to strengthen its defenses. Cuba would not even need an army. . . ."

This was said in advance. Anyone who wishes to may express doubts that Castro would carry out his end of this undertaking, but the point is that this was a decisive challenge to the United States. If Castro was bluffing, it would have been easy to call the bluff. All that Kennedy had to do was guarantee that he would not commit that which would be a war crime in any case, i.e., another invasion. What stopped him from giving such assurances?

As is well known, he not only refused to give such assurances but on the contrary allowed signs of quite different intentions. With incredible *gaucherie* or arrogance (I am not quite sure which), he even blurted out at a press conference that he did not favor an invasion *at this time.*

"What else could he have done?" Why, in the first place, promise not to commit the crime of invasion; hammer this home with suitable practical steps in Florida and elsewhere; dismantle what everybody knew were standby preparations and formations for invasion; publicly repudiate the invasion talk of the government-supported Cuban émigré phalanxes gathered in Miami like vultures; apply the law to catch and punish the émigré pirates using American facilities as a sanctuary from which to raid Cuba, and urge both Puerto Rico and Guatemala to do likewise; and several other things which the Invasion Planning Committee in Washington would have no difficulty in thinking of if it really wanted to convince Cuba and the world that any perspective of invasion or other military intervention was off. And then it would be up to Castro.

It is not a question merely of some empty promise not to invade. That is for diplomats, international lawyers and Stevensons. We are talking about a *political offensive.* The point of a political offensive is not merely to make the record, but to make an impact on the thinking and feeling of masses all over the world.

But this is pipedreaming as far as the Kennedy government is concerned. Such a political offensive on behalf of a *democratic anti-imperialist foreign policy* is foreign to it. To this day Kennedy has refused to give any real commitment against an invasion even though Khrushchev formally based his agreement to dismantle on such a commitment. Indeed, if and when Kennedy is ever compelled, despite squirming and twisting that Gromyko could be proud of, to give a real commitment against invasion, this will mean that Moscow has won a triumph.

"What else could he have done?" A different United States could have pursued a democratic anti-imperialist foreign policy. It can still do so. The means are right before it. There never was a better time to drive a wedge between the Cuban people (and even the Castro regime) and Moscow than now. The U.S. simply has to make clear that no matter what it thinks of the Castro regime, it is ceasing all arm twisting and coercion in relation to Cuba.

Then all it has to do is implement this position with deeds: like stopping all émigré raids, espionage and sabotage activities in Cuba,* ending its economic blockade and commercial strong-arm methods; desisting from further illegal air flights over Cuba or incursions into its waters; and, crowning measure, *proving* beyond all possibility of doubt that it has no remnant of intention to invade by withdrawing from its armed base on Cuban soil, Guantanamo, to which it has no right in the first place, and which is notoriously of no military importance in any case.

Now if Castro is a Communist, as we are told every day, and if the Cuban regime is a mere satellite of Moscow now, as the American Party Line has it, then these measures will not drive a wedge between Castro and Moscow, but *all the more will they drive a gulf between Castro and the Cuban people.* They will blow to smithereens any ability of Castro to "subvert" other Latin American countries with "lies about Yankee imperialism."

On the other hand, what does the U.S. lose by all this *if* it is not really interested in crushing the little country?

The reality of U.S. imperialism is concretized by the fact that all this, too, is pipedreaming as far as Washington is concerned. It is socially incapable of a democratic foreign policy.

Now the proposals listed above are, as the acute reader has noted, exactly the five proposals made by Castro himself in his speech of October 28. He made them knowing full well whom he was dealing with. But if a different United States were actually to implement them, this would be a bombshell right under Castro's seat.

And now we learn that a new blockade is being planned out by the strategists in Washington. We have mentioned that the U.S. camp is faced with the problem of how to react if Khrushchev chooses to harass it with a new Berlin blockade; that is, if he does to an enclave within Communist territory what the U.S. has done to an independent country outside its territory. Reports the New York *Times* from Washington in words that should send a chill through the country:

---

* A distinction should be made between democratic underground activities against the Castro regime and the sort of destructive sabotage, which can only alienate the Cuban people and be an appendage of U.S. intervention in Cuba. Anyone who talks about supporting a democratic underground is obligated to repudiate this kind of action very clearly.

> There is an agreement in principle [in NATO] that . . . [a Berlin blockade] should be met with strong Western actions up to and including an outright sea blockade of the whole Soviet bloc. . . .

> This would mean setting up naval pickets, similar to those around Cuba, to cut the principal sea routes to the Soviet Union and the East European Communist states . . . not even neutral shipping would be permitted to cross the lines. [But "selected cargoes" may be passed through.] [November 16.]

Will the eminent professors assure us that if we sink a few Russian ships, "there isn't anything Russia can do"?

It must also be remembered that this situation is most likely to eventuate, if it does eventuate, out of Khrushchev's threat to sign a peace treaty with East Germany, and turn over control of Western access to Berlin to the East German government, which the Western camp refuses to recognize. The same dispatch relates what the planners' thinking is if East German guards are substituted for Russians in controlling overland traffic to Berlin. This, it is says, "might bring the following response": the East German guards would be "seized bodily and delivered to the Russians as 'impostors'. "This in East German territory itself! "Another move might be to make an armed probe down the autobahn . . ." i.e., invade in force.

One of the most fantastic sides to U.S. foreign policy, even in this fantastic world, is the fact that it is the U.S. which *insists* that the Russian occupation remain astride East Germany. In a country whose people tried to drive the Russians out with unexampled courage in 1953, American armed forces are going to turn East German guards over to *their Russian masters* for daring to assert their independent authority. This is the dreamlike consequence of U.S. refusal to recognize or deal with East Germany independently, as it refuses also to recognize the existence of Communist China in order to build up the hand of the butcher Chiang Kai-shek. On this basis, no political offensive against the Communist world is possible.

This is the common denominator of U.S. foreign policy. Considering the U.S. as the bastion of beleaguered "free enterprise," i.e., capitalism, it knows only the military approach. But we are living in a world whose overwhelming majority, in all continents except North America, thinks of itself today as being for some kind of "socialism," at any rate hostile to the old system. All the new political ideas burgeoning in the world, agitating millions, permeating new countries and old in all kinds of ways, including distorted ways — all these ideas are alien to this "bastion of capitalism" mentality. Political ideas themselves become suspect, therefore, because anyone capable of getting ideas is likely to get the wrong ones. But you know where you are with guns, and only the most reactionary neanderthals in the world are politically reliable.

But if the American Party Line mind is incapable of a democratic *political offensive* against the Communist power, there is a considerable strain of its critics who are equally incapable of thinking in terms of any offensive against the Communist power. Desiring peace, and separating the struggle for peace from the social struggle at large, they are driven to interpret the Cold War as an unfortunate misunderstanding among misguided men, who are to be brought together by appeasing their groundless fears. Objectively, they may even find themselves standing for capitulation to the Kremlin, as they react in justified horror against the heavy-handed militarism of Washington.

These are not the alternatives between which we must choose. If they were, we would be lost. We do not have to choose either Kennedy's threats of nuclear war and military-oriented imperialistic policy, or an appeaser's program of keeping Moscow happy. There is a third way, pointed against both war camps, which proposes a democratic foreign policy, hence an anti-imperialist and anticapitalist foreign policy, based on a political offensive against the new exploitative system of Communist totalitarianism as well as the old exploitative system of capitalism.

New Politics
Fall 1962

The Revolutionary Potential in Vietnam

Introductory Note

This material constituted part of a pamphlet published by the Independent Socialist Club *on the campus of the University of California at Berkeley in 1966, that is, in the midst of the great student antiwar movement of those years. I suggested that it would be worthwhile getting the student antiwar protestors acquainted with what had happened in Vietnam a decade before, when the United States government, in one of its first of its crucial interventions, had stepped in to destroy the beginnings of a revolutionary movement in the country that at last had the* potential *of providing a Third Camp alternative to the old and oppressive warlords whom Washington was backing, on the one hand, and the North Vietnamese totalitarian regime on the other.*

I had written this up in May of 1955 in Labor Action: *and at a time when American leftists hardly even knew that the U.S. was already hip deep in Vietnam politics.* Labor Action *came out with a headline bigger than any we had run before: "HANDS OFF INDO-CHINA!" (I would claim priority for that one, in terms of the left press.) How this came about is worth retelling, for it bears on a point which is still operating. Not long before this, I had gone out on a speaking tour; and, in various cities, picked up whatever copies of the* New York Times *I could find. They turned out to be early editions, which I rarely if ever saw while living in New York. In a series of these editions of the* Times. *I read on inside pages the detailed dispatches sent in by the paper's correspondent(s) in Saigon, with astonishing reports, described firsthand, of political fermentation and dissent.* When I returned to New York, I found that my friends had seen none of these: they had disappeared from the final editions. *Evidently they had been regarded as filler for the early edition before the rest of the copy came in. To the best of my knowledge, also, the editions used for microfilm records and indexing were the final editions, without this material. The account I wrote up for* Labor Action *was of course based on this suppressed (or at least not* expressed*) material.*

This was, for the most part, the material which was summarized, in 1966, for the Independent Socialist Club *pamphlet. Perhaps all the original articles of 1955 should be reprinted in the present series, but this later summary is of value for now.*   H. D.

America as Overlord

1. *Revolt in the Cities, 1966*

There is a people's revolt in progress in the cities of South Vietnam, at this moment, directed against the American-supported government of General Ky and his fellow generals, and demanding a more democratic civilian regime instead of the dictatorship of the self-proclaimed admirer of Hitler who is Washington's Man in Saigon. This revolt, which has shaken and threatens to destroy the confidence of the American people in the Johnson Administration, is the most important new development in the Vietnamese struggle in the last decade.

That a popular democratic rebellion is in progress is clear from the press reports; but it is far less clear, of course, who the rebel leaders and forces are. We read about the leaders of two wings of the Buddhists, the militant leader of the left wing Tri Quang, and the moderate leader Tam Chau — who obviously wishes to come to an agreement with Ky but is pushed from below (from the left) to make demands which the government refuses to accept. We read that popular demonstrations in the streets are monitored by monks, although it seems that these monitor monks cannot always succeed in restraining the mass demonstrations which they may lead.

We suggest, however, that you should not necessarily adopt the conclusion that this is a religious movement. At bottom it is not, though there are clear reasons why it takes that form. In the history of Vietnamese nationalist movements, you find the phenomenon of religious sects which are at the same time political groups. Such politico-religious sects as the Cao Dai and the Hoa Hao have a record of functioning as political movements while at the same time their ideologies are framed in religious terms. Of course, the Cao Dai's religion was a synthetic one, and the Hoa Hao's religion is a sort of deviant Buddhism; whereas the two Buddhist leaders who are most prominently involved now are from the official church. But that's what happens under repression. We must understand that South Vietnam has been living under a series of American-dominated dictatorships, beginning with Diem's regime in 1954, which systematically destroyed political opposition groups. It is typical of situations like this that oppositional tendencies — denied the right to organize politically — flow into other forms, into channels that are still permitted.

We have seen the same thing happen in the American civil rights movement, particularly in the South, were the Black Churches — the only independent organizations of Black people — became the original organizing centers for political struggle, *despite* the conservatism of the ministers. And at bottom what we are seeing now is an outbreak of the irrepressible desire for political expression by the people through the channels of existing religious institutions, since political channels are denied by the Ky regime.

But clearly — still going by the press reports, such as they are — there is more going on than what is manifested through the Buddhist organizational forms. There are plainly mass student movements in the field, of at least a semi-organized nature. There may be other organizational forces. For example, in April, the *San Francisco Chronicle* carried a N.Y. *Times* dispatch from Da Nang, which had the following towards its close about a resolution:

> The validity of the anti-Ky resolution circulated here was difficult for Western journalists to check. The resolution, asserting that the "entire" staff of the First Corps would struggle for Ky's downfall, was brought to the Da Nang press billet along with 15 pages of typed names and signatures of officers. . . .
>
> It appeared likely that a considerable number of officers had signed the resolution, but that it was not a military document. Apparently the petition has been initiated by antigovernment political forces operating in the area.

One of the striking things about this situation is how far — how very, very far — the Western journalists seem to be from having the least idea of what is happening among the people. Movements of tens of thousands of people take place, and the picture we get is as if by a man light years away viewing it all through a telescope (with a dirty lens).

According to this dispatch, there are antigovernment political forces operating, in some organized form, which clearly is not the Vietcong — which gets the signatures of a whole officer cadre of the army — and not only do the Western journalists know nothing about it, they can find nothing out about it, *or they are not interested in doing so;* and we would remind you that the decision makers in Washington, as in the American embassy in Saigon, are undoubtedly just as much in the dark or uninterested. Between them, and the mass of the people of South Vietnam, is a *chasm*.

For us — and we would recommend that it be for you too — there is nothing more important to find out, to know about. What is happening now is happening for the first time in South Vietnam since 1955. It marks, or can mark, a brand new stage in the Vietnam war. It can be a new beginning for that tortured country (though we are far from being optimistic at this point). To understand the *possibilities* though, is also to understand more clearly the nature of this war.

This is the first time since 1955 that a popular-democratic rebellion has taken open, organized form directed against the American-sponsored government on the one hand, and independent of the Communist opposition on the other. What has happened regularly in Vietnam is this: as disgust with the government and with American intervention has risen, this disgust and disillusionment and hatred has been pushed into the arms of the Vietcong, as the only alternative. Support for the Vietcong, or toleration of it, has not been the result of the great attractive powers of Communism, but — quite otherwise — has been a consequence of the sins and crimes of a series of reactionary regimes which Washington's interventionist forces have leaned on. The Vietcong owes everything to the United States — which is its Secret Weapon. As long as the Communists are the only alternative, there is an unending and unbreakable source of popular support for the Vietcong forces; this is the political secret of their ability to stand off the overwhelmingly superior military forces of the strongest power on earth.

What the present rebellion signifies then, is a thrust toward a different alternative — a third road which points to a popular-democratic regime independent of the Communists and their agents. We say, this is the *possibility* that it points to, although obviously we cannot evaluate its probability in a situation which changes from day to day, and on the basis of unreliable press reporting.

Now there is nothing that frightens our great democratic American leaders so much as the very idea of an independent Third Force with popular-democratic aspirations. If your sense of humor is ghoulish enough, you ought to be dying of laughter at the spectacle of the Washington officials, like William Bundy, who are officially claiming to be neutral in this conflict, while at the same time falling all over themselves with eagerness to help the military government extricate itself from this assault by the people. You should admire the public relations technique of President Johnson, who deplores the "unnecessary" fire suicides of Buddhist monks — he is not as crude as Madame Nhu, who "clapped her hands" at the sight of "monk barbecues".

According to various news reports, the State Department is so "neutral" that it even has a position on the Buddhist factions — it's supporting the moderate monks against the militant monks; and of course we saw how U.S. airplanes were used to airlift General Ky's troops to Da Nang.

American policy is reflected by the imbecile who wrote an editorial in the *San Francisco Chronicle* (during the April demonstrations) which ended with this precious paragraph:

> Meanwhile, the disorder and jockeying for power and lack of popular discipline contribute nothing whatever to a belief in this long-troubled people's ability to govern themselves when and if peace comes.

Imagine that: Here we Americans have imposed a government of reactionary generals whom the people never had a say in naming; and when a mass movement arises asking just for elections of a civilian government — and has to call demonstrations in order to pres these reactionary generals to listen to such a demand — this voice of American democracy chides them:"Now, now, you Vietnamese people, this lack of popular discipline shows you are incapable of governing yourselves."

Well, that is the Standard American Mind; but what our great American democrats are really afraid of, of course, is that a truly independent regime in Saigon would refuse to continue the war which is wrecking and ruining the country. They're afraid not that the Vietnamese can't govern themselves, but that the Vietnamese intend to govern themselves without the Americans around to burn and blow up the countryside.

Now if there is any hope at all for an independent future for Vietnam, here is where it lies. We do not know, and we cannot know reassure you, how great that hope may be; it might not work at all; but what we are quite sure of is that in any other direction there is no hope for an independent democratic Vietnam at all.

If a genuinely popular-democratic government were set up in South Vietnam, we are quite sure that it would move to a negotiated peace at the least, if not the immediate withdrawal of U.S. troops; and the next stage would be a political tug-of-war. Taken at its best, such a popular government could win back at least the non-Communist components of the National Liberation Front — those elements who are with the Vietcong now only because they do not see any other alternative. Such a popular government could then try to work our the problem of some *modus vivendi* with Hanoi. All this would be a rocky road, with no guarantee of a happy outcome; but without it, there is no doubt that the future of South Vietnam is simply absorption by the Communists or obliteration in unending destruction.

Both the Americans and the Communists will be bitterly opposed to such a new line of development. We can't do much about the Communists' opposition, which will try to exploit and take over the popular movement, but as Americans it is our responsibility to do our damndest to checkmate our government's sabotage of the glimmerings of Vietnamese democracy.

2. The Revolutionary Committees 1955.

The United States was instrumental in destroying a popular-democratic movement once in Vietnam before. In May of 1955, there took place an upsurge *similar to what is happening now* in many respects: similar in that the center of the political stage was taken by emerging political forces that were neither in the camp of the Western imperialists nor in the camp of the Communists. (This episode, by the way, has been equally ignored in the chronicles of the Vietnam story, both by the pro-Americans and the pro-Communists: and unfortunately it was also ignored in Bob Scheer's very useful pamphlet, "How the United States Got Involved in Vietnam".)

Here was the situation in April — May 1965 when this happened. At the same time, the victory of the Communist Vietminh as Dienbienphu, and the settlement at the Geneva conference had given the northern part of Vietnam to Ho Chi Minh, who still had considerable support in the South too. In the middle of the following year (1956) there was going to be a national plebiscite (supposedly); and as early as this, every observer expected the Communists to win hands down. For what was the alternative regime in the South?

The Chief of State was still Bao Dai — the handpicked Emperor of the French — who spent most of his time sunning himself on the Riviera (the French Riviera). But the French were on the way out (though their troops were still in the country), and one of the first steps in the process whereby America was taking over from the French, was their installation of their own man as a premier (under Bao Dai). This was Ngo Dinh Diem.

Now it is true (as Scheer relates in his pamphlet) that the U.S. adopted Diem, in part, because it thought that Diem could garner Third Force sentiment in the country, and perhaps stand a chance of winning the vote. Certainly he was better able than France's handmade Emperor to make an appeal to such Third force sentiment — to people who wanted to support *neither* the Communists nor Western stooges.

But insofar as Diem had such a Third Force appeal, it was a demagogic appeal — it was nothing but a fraud. For the last thing that the U.S. wanted was a real Third Force in power — a Third force in the only meaningful sense: one that was really *independent* of the Communist powers and the Western powers.

Such a genuine independent Third Force only in one way: through *revolution*. And where would that come form? From whom? As usual, on the very eve of a mass revolutionary upsurge from below, from among the masses of people, all of the authorities and experts scoffed at the very idea.

As an alternative to the Communists, Diem very soon showed himself a flop. It is not true (as one reads here and there) that in his first year or two Diem pushed a progressive social policy and only became a reactionary later. What is true is that in his first year, Diem paid *lip service* to the goal of land reform, and so on. But at every point, he compromised with the ruling circles of landowners, usurers, bloodsuckers and compradores of all kinds who lived off the people. He did nothing to create really representative government. He had a reputation for being personally honest, but what good was that, when on every social issue Diem went along with the class from which he himself derived?

True, he was pulling away from the *French*; but only to convince everybody that he was the chief instrument for substituting the rule of the dollar for the franc.

Very soon it was clear that few Vietnamese could be very happy voting for this government as against Ho Chih Minh, who was still a national hero, with the great prestige of the victory over the French. This was no Third Force alternative — no attractive alternative of any kind.

The crisis came, however, as a result of a squeeze play engineered by the French. The French colonialists, by this time, hated the Americans who were squeezing them out of Vietnam as much as the Communists. (So reported American journalists in Saigon.) They were still capable of ingenious foul plays. They bitterly told the Americans that this man of theirs, Diem, could not do the job, that his government would only bring chaos; and to prove it, they didn't mind manufacturing the chaos themselves.

To this end, one of the last acts of the French puppet regime preceding Diem had been to put the police force of Saigon into the hands of a gang known as the Binh Xuyen, which had its own private army. This was not one of the religious sects! It was commonly referred to as river pirates, but it was a criminal gang with wider interests, especially murder (Murder INc.), prostitution, and dope smuggling.

The Diem government therefore had no real police force of its own, and the army was a very uncertain quantity, particularly because of the French. When Diem moved to fire the police chief (the Bien Xuyen man) and to take other steps against allied corrupt and criminal elements, he found himself in deep trouble. A veritable war broke out between the government and this Murder Inc. which expected and got help from the French, whose troops were still in Saigon. The French forces hampered the operations of Diem's men as much as possible, while giving free rein to the whore-and-dope peddlers. While this battle was going on in the streets of Saigon, Paris issued statements demanding that Diem show his ability to govern by making peace with these Patriots; and at press conferences they came out with blasts against Diem for "dividing the nation's forces", and so on. As this fantastic battle went on, it looked as if Diem was tottering. There were even indications that the Americans were beginning to accept the French line, that Diem could not "handle the situation", etc. — just as the French had planned.

At this juncture, a new force took the field. This was a wave of Revolutionary Committees that sprang up all over the country, from the grass roots. At the end of April, Diem had warned Bao Dai that "secret revolutionary committees" were coming into being in the provinces, and that if he (Bao Dai) continued to excite the army and the population as he was doing, a revolution would sweep the country. This was a warning.

On May 1st, Diem had to negotiate directly with the Revolutionary Committee. During May 1st and 2nd, a planned coup (against Diem) by General Vy was thrown back, but only by the direct intervention of the Revolutionary Committee. At one point, the press actually reported that General Vy had control of the palace and Diem had been ousted. A few hours later, the Revolutionary Committee stepped onto the stage publicly for the first time (according to the reporters' first hand accounts.) Right in the palace, with General Vy a virtual prisoner, it was the head of the Revolutionary Committee that read out the manifesto announcing the deposition of Bao Dai and calling for a new government. They were demanding a republic, independence, and free elections.

This spokesman for the Revolutionary Committee was its president, Nguyen Bao Tanh, named in the *Times* dispatch as secretary of a new political party formed by the left wing of the Hoa Hao group, calling itself the Social

Democratic Party (not the same as the Socialist Party of Vietnam, which was also a component of the Revolutionary Committee).

Now, after back the anti-Diem coup, the Revolutionary Committee started to drive ahead to extend its power — that is, to go beyond Diem too. It called a Congress in Saigon to meet May 5th, a few days away — the National Revolutionary Congress — to effectuate the call for a republic. This congress met, and on May 6th here is what the *New York Times* dispatch from Saigon reported, as it described the whole capital in ferment:

> The day was one of confused and frenzied political activity. Meetings, speechmaking, demonstrations and excited comings and goings went on around the clock. . . .

> The bigger and wilder of today's political congresses was one sponsored by a group that calls itself the People's National Revolutionary Committee. Under the direction of the Committee, 4000 representatives of 95 political parties and branch revolutionary committees from all over the southern half of Vietnam met. . . .
> After having heard speeches against Bao Dai, colonialism and communism and debated the issues for eight hours, the revolutionary congress ended the day by adopting a set of principles and an action program. . . .

> The principles called for unity among all the nationalist forces of the country, refusal of all power to Bao Dai, the strengthening of South Vietnam against communism, collaboration with anticommunist, anticolonialist and antifeudal forces throughout Southeast Asia, and the establishment of a nationalist-socialist-democratic regime for South Vietnam.

Among those in the Congress were figures who had broken away from the Communist Vietminh in reaction to its totalitarianism, and who were trying to build a democratic revolutionary alternative, in alliance with the political left of all kinds and the left wing of the religious-political sects. This was a very broad left front, against both Western colonialism and Communism.

Very broad, very heterogeneous, and there was also its weakness; for there was no hard, experienced revolutionary leadership around; and it is very difficult to make a successful revolution without that.

141

For naturally, Diem — with revolution breathing down his neck — was capable of a few maneuvers himself. For the same May 5th, he had called another congress, the National Political Congress, made up of councilors from the provinces who were mainly his own men (and in any case not mixed up with the Revolutionary Committees). Even in this assemblage of moderates and "notables" , a majority wanted to get rid of Bao Dai, and a strong wing wanted an immediate republic. American reporters noted that American officials were warning Diem that this Congress of his had better not get out of hand.

It was the American representatives — specifically, President Eisenhower's special envoy, General Collins — who set their faces against dumping Bao Dai. Collins announced that he favored a constitutional monarchy for Vietnam! "How are these poor people going to run a republic?" said Collins. "We even have trouble doing it in the United States sometimes." *New York Times* correspondent Homer Bigart reported that although the U.S. had no love for Bao Dai, they now tended to see him as the only thread of "legality" — i.e., as the safeguard against revolution.

In this situation, one of the acts of the Revolutionary Congress was to declare its support of Diem *to carry out its program*. The pattern is that of the Russian Revolution, after March, looking to Prince Lvov and Kerensky to carry out the revolutionary process.

But this revolution had less opportunity to develop further. General Collins saw to that. It was the pressure of the Americans, and particularly their threats to cut off all aid and money to Vietnam, that eased the pressure on Diem, and made it possible for him to gradually get rid of the revolutionary threat. In the course of the ensuing period, Diem and his men systematically rooted out all political opposition, and filled the jails with opponents, establishing an increasingly repressive dictatorship. It is beyond doubt that in this way, many of the elements in the Revolutionary Committees were driven into the arms of the only remaining alternative, the Communists; and this helped to bring about the rise of the Vietcong and the tragedies of the next decade.

Now it is 1966, and again an independent popular-democratic revolt arises in South Vietnam against America's man. The question is: *will the United States again succeed in strangling this revolutionary hope?*

Berkeley
1969

The ABC of National Liberation Movements
A Political Guide

Introductory Note

This document — a political discussion guide — was written for the members of the Independent Socialist Club *of Berkeley when the Vietnam War seemed to take a new turn, with the Tet offensive of 1968 launched by the National Liberation Front. For the Independent Socialists, the turn did not entail a different attitude toward the United States' intervention as world overlord of the capitalist bloc. The club had long been in the forefront of the anti-Vietnamese war movement in Berkeley.*

In my opinion, what the Tet offensive showed, with no possibility of doubt any longer, was that the war in Vietnam was not primarily a civil war *between two Vietnamese sides, one of which (the old reactionary side) was being supported by the imported arms of the Western imperialists. The Tet offensive showed conclusively that the overwhelming majority of the Vietnamese supported the NLF either actively or passively. The document below explains how this makes a difference, and what difference it makes — not to the question of support to the American intervention, but to one's interpretation of the role of the NLF.*

Besides, even aside from this factor, there was a need for educational analysis of a number of issues associated with national liberation movements in general. Many of the members of the Independent Socialist Club *were young people who had never before faced complicated problems of socialist policy; this antiwar movement was the first time they had been brought up against such needs. The Independent Socialists were outstanding in combining the most militant opposition to the American government in the war together with a refusal to glorify the NLF and its leader Ho Chi Minh. This required a good deal of thinking through on their part, as distinct from chanting paeans of praise to the political force that was going to totalitarianize Vietnamese society if it won.*

This "political guide" was designed for study and discussion. It was written in the form of (to use socialist jargon), a "set of theses." The point about "theses" is to state, in as clear and unambiguous a manner as possible, a position on a more or less complicated question. The aim of "theses" is not necessarily to prove a case, but primarily to state it in unmistakable terms. The young socialists of the Club had heard many things about socialist policy in national liberation situations: the idea was to try to put it all together.

H.D.

1. *Anti-imperialism and Revolution*

As revolutionary socialists in the U.S. our immediate enemy is American capitalism and its imperialism; and we wish to fight American capitalism at home and American imperialism abroad by every available means.

At bottom this is a single fight, since any weakening of American imperialism abroad or defeat suffered by it abroad also weakens the domestic capitalist power structure and facilitates opposition at home. The same is also true for other imperialist states, since a weakening or defeat of one or another power reverberates through the interconnected structure of world imperialism.

Therefore, *objectively*, anti-imperialist struggle by any people is an aid to the forces of revolutionary change at home.

But a warning is necessary: that word "objectively" represents a famous pitfall.

(a) It is one thing to analyze and understand the objective effect of an event, and quite another thing to leap to the conclusion that we therefore advocate it or support it. We do not advocate depression, war or superexploitation on the ground that they stimulate revolution.

(b) An event may have more than one objective effect; this is a risky way of arriving at a policy. In our present world, specific victories by American imperialism may have the objective effect of weakening Communist imperialism, and vice versa; but as an enemy of both, we do not find this an adequate basis for deciding policy. It is one consideration, to be taken in context. There is no substitute for concreteness.

Whenever anti-imperialist resistance breaks out into armed struggle, our attitude toward that war is based on the same fundamental consideration as our attitude on any other war, viz:

A war is politics continued by other, that is forcible, means. Our attitude toward a war must be congruent with our attitude toward the politics of which it is the continuation. This determines our principled position on the question of whether to support or oppose a given war — not primarily our opinion of the men, the government or the class leading the war, not our opinion of their past or present crimes. The latter considerations will be very relevant to *how* we support or oppose a war, but not to *whether* we do.

If an armed struggle is decisively a continuation of resistance to imperialist oppression, then it is decisively a war of national liberation that deserves the support of revolutionary socialists.

144

2. *National Elements and Imperialist Elements*

It is true that a particular national struggle can be swallowed up in, and overshadowed by, a more all-embracing conflict of an imperialist character, so that it is impossible to support any side of the national struggle without supporting one or another side in the general war

The case of Serbia. Such a case, in fact, was seen at the very beginning of World War I, which was triggered by the national struggle of the Serbs against the Hapsburg Empire.

If that conflict had remained on the ground of the antagonism between the Serbian people and its imperialist oppressor, revolutionary socialists would have been prowar, i.e. *pro* the national war of the Serbs. But in fact the Serbian struggle was completely integrated into the Allied camp; and this national *element* in a predominantly imperialist was therefore outweighed.

The case of Spain. A different case was exemplified by the Spanish Civil War. (We are not citing it as a war of national liberation; we wish to make a point common to both civil wars and wars of national liberation.)

In the case of Spain, Marxists supported the military defense of the loyalist regime, since in their view this civil war was decisively a continuation of the politics of *the defense of the democratic republic against a fascist assault* — that is, it was *really* a conflict between democracy and fascism, not demagogically so, like the previous war to "make the world safe for democracy." While other aspects of policy will be considered later, we point out here that it was clear in Spain there was an international imperialist *element* in this conflict. German and Italian military units even fought on Franco's side; foreign socialists and Communists organized to fight on the loyalist side; Russia intervened nonmilitarily on a large scale; a web of diplomatic imperialist maneuvering went on around the tragic situation. In fact, the Spanish war was a localized hot war in the midst of an international imperialist Cold War. It was quite possible that World War II could have been triggered off by it, and this eventuality would have completely overshadowed and changed the character of the local war, as in the case of Serbia. But it did not and this remained only a potentiality, not a fact; and therefore the Marxists' attitude of military support did not have to change.

The conclusion is: the existence of an international context of imperialist antagonism (Cold War) is inevitably *reflected* in almost any conceivable local conflict, and may give rise to imperialist *elements* in any local situation, but it does not thereby necessarily *determine the character* of that local conflict.

3. Why Socialists Support National Liberation

How does support to a war of national liberation relate to the basic politics of revolutionary socialism? In two ways:

(1) The first restates the point we have just made about our basic approach: the politics of which war is a continuation. We support a struggle for a national liberation or independence because this national aim is a *democratic demand.*

We are for *all* genuinely democratic demands — for the same reason we are for socialist demands and aims: because their fulfillment is necessary for a world in which human potentialities can best flower. National self-determination is a democratic demand even if it means self-determination under an undemocratic national government, as it often has. We should support this democratic demand even if it were unrelated to the further struggle for socialist democracy.

(2) But, as a matter of fact, it is very difficult if not impossible for any genuinely democratic demand to be unrelated to the struggle for socialism, because of the nature of socialism itself. National liberation (independence) *facilitates* the struggle for socialist democracy, if not immediately then in a later stage.

The essential reason is this: domination or oppression from the outside by a foreign imperialist tends to overlay the social struggle class struggle) of the indigenous society, and therefore to distort, dampen or moderate precisely those social antagonisms which bear a social revolutionary potential. A people who do not enjoy national freedom will tend to primary attention to *that* immediate source of pain; their capacity to struggle will tend to be dominated by it; their perception of who-is-the-enemy will tend to be dominated by it. Therefore imperialist oppression tends to set back or slow up a full crystallization and clarification of *class* antagonisms; and a liberation from imperialist domination will have the long run effect of providing the conditions for the exacerbation of internal class strains (even if the *immediate* effect of a national liberation victory appears to be otherwise for an initial period). This is not gainsaid by the fact that, to be sure, revolutionary policy aims to introduce class struggle components even in the course of a national struggle.

Here, as in other sectors of politics, the fight for democracy includes specifically the democratic demand for, national liberation.

4. *Military Support and Political Support*

Besides the question of *whether* to support a given war, it is vital to be clear on *how* revolutionary socialists support a war. A distinctive feature of the Marxist approach is the distinction between *military support* of a given armed struggle and *political support* to a given political organization including a government) which may be officially "in charge" of that armed struggle.

This pregnant distinction goes far back in the marxist movement, perhaps the first prominent example being Bebel and Liebknecht's refusal to vote for war funds for the Franco-Prussian war. It has never been more important than today.

For most people, including liberals, social democrats and opportunists of every stripe, "support" means support, period. For Marxists, it never has. This is one reason why, not infrequently, political leaders of a national struggle have been almost as unhappy about being supported by revolutionists as by being opposed. Typically, the official leaders demand "civil peace" below in the ranks of their supporters, by which they mean unquestioning acceptance of their own dominance; they call for the end of "partisan politics," by which they mean they want unquestioning support of their own partisan politics.

But Marxists see no more reason to give *political* support — to a government, to a party, or to any other political organization — in wartime than in peacetime, and do not believe that basic differences in social policy become irrelevant just because policy is to be carried out by arms rather than by "normal" means.

On the contrary, it is precisely *basic* (especially, class) differences in social policy which may make the difference between victory or defeat in the armed struggle itself (as in the Spanish case), or may determine just what it is that is won and who does the winning, after victory is achieved.

5. *Six Cases*

Let us take three pairs of cases to illustrate some problems of military and political support, especially in national wars.

(1:A) The Case of Chiang Kai Shek vs. Japan. This refers to the period before World War II when Japanese imperialism was carrying on a blatantly aggressive policy, grabbing Manchuria and threatening to take over all China.

At the head of the Chinese resistance government was, officially, Chiang Kai Shek and his Kuomintang — who, not long before, had distinguished themselves by their counter revolutionary fury in a bloodthirsty suppression of the working class in the cities. Internationally, socialists (and others) gave military support to the Chiang regime as against the Japanese invaders — even Chinese revolutionaries who simultaneously had to defend themselves more against Chiang's butchers than against the Japanese. And this, for a regime (Chiang's) which could not be said to represent a bourgeois democratic social force, being not very bourgeois and even less democratic.

(1:B) The Case of Ethiopia vs. Italy. Mussolini's openly imperialist attack on the realm of Haile Selasie was a similar case. The society ruled by the Negus was an incredibly reactionary one (not capitalist reaction but precapitalist reaction) — real slavery being by no means its most objectionable feature. In comparison, even Fascist Italy was a more progressive society, it goes without saying. Yet socialists gave unquestioned support to the defense of Ethiopia against this "more progressive society," and even the Communists were embarrassed by Russia's treacherous sale of badly needed oil to Mussolini's war machine.

Why the support? Ethiopian society was so reactionary that not everything we have said about the reasons for supporting national wars can possibly apply. Most particularly, a victorious defense by Ethiopia could hardly be expected to be very relevant to "facilitating social revolution" in that country; in fact, a case could be made that Italian conquest would probably create revolutionary elements in Ethiopia more quickly.

The essential justification must be sought in two statements:

(a) The national freedom of Ethiopia was a *democratic* demand, as already explained; and

(b) a successful conquest of Ethiopia by Mussolini would have had a definitely retrogressive meaning for the social struggle *in Italy*, by helping to consolidate fascism internally, with a derivative similar effect elsewhere in Europe.

(2:A) The Spanish Civil War. We are here interested in the difference between military and political support in this situation.

Revolutionary socialists could not give *political* support to the bourgeois republican government which had been attacked by Franco.

This republican government had itself brutally shot down militant workers only the day before yesterday,. Moreover, it was an imperialist government, so much so that not even the need to win over Franco's Moorish troops, in order to save its own neck, was enough to get it to declare for freeing Morocco. Revolutionary socialists could have no confidence in the conduct of the war by the section of the republican bourgeoisie which had not gone over to Franco, not even confidence in their will to fight Franco to the end, and certainly no confidence in their ability to fight Franco by the only means that could win, revolutionary means. When, in a later stage, due to Russian pressure exercised through material aid, Communist Party influence in the government became strong, to the point where the Spanish section of the GPU even had its own jails, the government apparatus was indeed used to silence and murder revolutionary opponents.

The military support to the struggle by the revolutionary left took the form of building *independent fighting forces* (the anarchist columns and POUM battalions), under their own command, while collaborating militarily with the forces of the government.

The existence of these independent armed forces of the left represented *the possibility of an alternative leadership* for the struggle as a whole; it reflected a basically different aim in the struggle itself (carrying over the struggle against Franco to social revolution, not a return to the discredited bourgeois status quo ante). The counter revolutionary character of the Loyalist government and its Communist allies was acted out when they turned on the independent left forces in a bloody suppression. This was a prelude to the defeat of the Loyalist forces themselves by Franco, since only social revolution could have defeated fascism in Spain.

In Spain, therefore, we see that military support of one camp in the war did not exclude the formation of independent armed forces to carry on the military struggle without subordinating it to the political control of the "official" leadership of the Loyalist camp. Similarly, outside of Spain, revolutionary socialists who sympathized with the left sent their material aid not to agencies of the official government but rather attempted to channel it as much as possible to the independent detachments, without opposing other efforts which were organized to send material aid to the Loyalist government.

(2:B) The Case of Algeria. There was no question but that revolutionary socialists supported the struggle of the Algerian people to free themselves from French imperialism. But for several years, the situation was characterized by the fact that there were *two* fighting movements of Algerian national liberation, neither of them "official": the FLN and the MNA. Supporters of Algerian liberation then had to choose between supporting one or the other (or both). Here military support automatically posed a problem in political support.

Here too, as in Spain, there was an element of Communist influence in the picture, since the Communists backed the FLN and influenced its operations, though the leadership of the FLN was not derived from the Communist movement. Here too terrorism and assassination was used by one movement (the FLN) against the other. As we know, the FLN succeeded in eliminating its rival for hegemony in the national liberation movement, and, after victory, established the new Algerian government. We believe that Marxists would have to be a revolutionary democratic opposition to that government, not its political supporters. The new government's politics were a continuation of its war (by other means). Political support to the FLN was by no means indicated merely by military support to the Algerian struggle for national liberation.

In this case, as in the case of Spain, there was a choice of political sides offered concretely, and therefore also a choice of *how* to give military support — through what *political* channels.

(3:A) Tito vs. Russia in 1948. We now come to two cases of a considerably different sort. In both cases the political power inviting support is a Communist government.

The first case of this new type was the situation created in 1948 when Tito's Yugoslavia broke with Moscow and set out on an independent national-Communist course.

There was widespread expectation that Russia would invade the country militarily to force it into line (as it did later in Hungary); there is every reason to believe that this was a real possibility, even though it never actually happened. It was necessary for socialists to be clear in their own midst what their attitude would be in the event of such a war — which would clearly be a continuation of Yugoslavia's move for national independence from Russia.

Independent Socialists stated promptly, at the time, that they would be for the military defense of Yugoslavia against such a Russian invasion. It goes without saying that there could be no question of political support to the Tito regime.

Nor, for that matter, could the Tito regime be expected to tolerate any independent forces within its borders even in support of its struggle; in time of war crisis, an independent force would be even more dangerous to its totalitarian control than before. If such a war had actually broken out, it is possible that its control would have loosened perforce and in spite of its aims, but this is speculative. In any case, military support of the Yugoslavian fight for national independence would not be *conditioned* on such development.

Why was military support to the Tito regime mandatory in this case? For all the reasons given above, but one of them must now be restated. This is the motivation which said: "National liberation facilitates the struggle for socialist democracy, *if not immediately then in a later stage.*" In what sense would victory for the Tito regime in such a war have facilitated the necessary "second revolution" in Yugoslavia? Not necessarily in the sense that the national war would itself merge into a social war, or immediately open the door to it. But certainly in this sense: that the other outcome, conquest by Russia, would mean the overlaying of the internal social antagonisms by the national question, and tend to blanket the former by the latter, thus delaying the reckoning.

What this means concretely was seen eight years later in Poland (1956) when an incipient national and social revolution combined was short circuited by Gomulka, essentially through the strategy of *counterposing* the national question to the social. A nationally independent Poland at that point would have lain open to social revolution.

History cannot guarantee when the "later stage" will arrive, but we know from all experience that the weight of national oppression is a weight that militates against the resolving of the social struggle by revolutionary means; and that this is fully as true of the bureaucratic collectivist regimes as of the capitalist.

In addition, we must insist that national independence is a *democratic demand* for countries under Communist rule, not less than for countries under the rule of feudal emperors and Kuomintang butchers.

(3:B) The Case of the Cuban Invasion. Whereas the danger in 1948 was the invasion of one Communist state by another Communist state, in 1961 we saw a Communist dominated state, Castro's, under the gun of an invasion sponsored by, and effectively organized under the aegis of, American imperialism. In point of fact the struggle was a brief one, since the U.S. pulled back after initial defeat, but it would be useful to consider this case as it would have been if the fighting had gone on for a period of time , in order to under-line the problems of policy.

American revolutionary socialists were duty-bound to condemn, and wish for the defeat of, the U.S. invasion of Cuba. Any vacillation or uncertainty on this point can only be regarded as a fundamental concession to the ideology of social patriotism.

We must especially reject the reasoning which makes the pervasive U.S.-Russian cold war the political determinant of the character of this 1961 conflict, that is, which makes it only a subordinate incident in the U.S.-Russian confrontation. This line of reasoning would wipe out almost *any* case of self-determination in the modern world — for example, the CIA-sponsored in-vasion of Guatemala in 1954 no less than the 1961 Cuban invasion. It has far less of a leg to stand on than the similar sectarian view which refused to sup-port the Loyalist camp in Spain on the ground that the civil war was only the first battle of World war II; for there actually were substantial foreign troops in Spain, whereas there was no Russian military force in Cuba whatsoever. The decisive political criterion must still be: concretely, what politics was *this* war the continuation of?

The right of Cuba (or any other country) to self-determination has absolutely nothing to do with whether we or anyone else approve of its government. This is, as we said, a democratic demand even under an undemocratic government. We would like to, see the Castro regime overthrown *by the Cuban people* in favor of a regime of socialist democracy, but this task cannot be contracted out to American imperialism, which is interested only in installing a regime subservient to world capitalism.

The conquest of Cuba by the U.S. would only have served to confirm American imperialism in its conviction that it not only has the right to police the world in favor of capitalism, but that it can do so successfully and with impunity; and this conviction could only lead to more and more extensive "police actions" of the Vietnam type. The consequence of this development could only be increased reaction at home — that is, if the U.S. succeeded in getting away with it.

Finally, in the case of Cuba as in the case of Tito, national independence "facilitates the struggle for socialist democracy, if not immediately then in a later stage." Conquest by the U.S. would not have convinced the Cuban people that Castro was a totalitarian dictator, but rather would have made him their national revolutionary hero defending Cuban integrity against them American colossus. This is exactly the pattern of how Ho Chi Minh captured the status of national hero of the Vietnamese people in the struggle against the French.

The struggle in Cuba for revolutionary democracy under socialism must take place under conditions of independence if it is to develop in a "later stage"; it can only be set back by U.S. domination. Even after the failure of the U.S. invasion and still today, the Castro regime uses the danger and fear of the U.S. intervention to promote support from the people on patriotic grounds.

We were and are therefore in favor of military support of the Castro regime against U.S. invasion, but, as before, this provides no reason whatsoever to convince us to give Castro *political* support, any more than we do now. We remain political opponents of the Castro dictatorship.

6. A Summary of Policy

Political support to an organization or movement or government (which means, its leadership) into political power. It is the equivalent of voting for this leadership if an election were to take place.

Political support to an organization or government heading a national struggle is essentially determined by the same considerations as if there were an unarmed political struggle going on (as there may have been before the armed phase of the struggle broke out). We cannot take an attitude of political opposition in the earlier phase and then switch to political support simply because the political war has been continued by other means.

We do not give political support simply because an organization or government demonstrates it has mass support. We do not give political support simply because an organization or government is an enemy of our enemy. We certainly do not give political support to a government simply because it is in power or gets into power. We do not give political support to a movement or government simply because it adopts a formal political program that is superficially unobjectionable. We do not give political support to a movement simply because it succeeds in inveigling the support of better political elements than its leadership. *We can give political support only on the basis of what we analyze as the real political character and real political program this formation, as in any other case.*

7. Military Support

Military support means that we prefer the military victory of one side in an armed struggle and the military defeat of the opposing side. This is as much a *political position as is an attitude of political support,* that is, it is determined by political considerations, not military ones. We have already summarized what those political causes are, and have applied them to various cases, where we prefer the military victory of a camp which we do not support politically.

Since the question of military support is a question of a political position, it raises the issue of *how* to give military support and to whom — that is, the implementing question of the forms of *material support.* It goes without saying that not every political position we take can be implemented at the time. Even though we frequently cannot implement political positions we take (as when we say we are for a labor party), the point of taking them is propagandistic, rather than a matter of agitation or action.

With respect to the implementation of military support, a major role is obviously played not simply by *our* attitude but by theirs, that is, the leadership of the national struggle in question. Is that national struggle led by a national democratic movement of some sort, or by nationalist authoritarian or totalitarian leaders?

A simple example: Are the leaders of that nationalist struggle as anxious to kill *you* as they are to kill the imperialist enemy? In most of the six cases we considered, it was in fact impossible for revolutionary forces to establish a relationship of peaceful coexistence and collaboration with the official leaders of the national struggle, and in some cases the latter would give higher priority to the task of physical extermination of a *revolutionary alternative to their own leadership* than to fighting the common foe.

This means it is impossible for the revolutionary to *openly* establish an independent fighting force to carry on military struggle, or that this can be done only in areas not controlled by the official leadership. Depending on the politics of the situation, "military support" may remain mainly a matter of a *political position* if there is no way to implement it without handing the revolutionary left over to the hangmen.

8. Three Situations

The concretization of military support is conditioned by which of the three types of situation exists with relation to the scene of the actual struggle:

(A) A movement in the *oppressed* country.

(B) A movement in the *oppressor* country, or in an ally of the oppressor.

(C) A movement in an uninvolved country.

It is only in situation A that revolutionary socialists concretely face the tactical problem of whether or not, and in what form, it is feasible to organize military support through independent forces, legal or illegal.

In situation B — a typical one for American revolutionists — we primarily have the task of politically implementing the position of *defeatism* which is the other side of the coin of military support of the national liberation struggle.

In both B and C, revolutionary socialists will try to determine whether it is possible or desirable to give *material aid* to any particular fighting force in the situation, and how to do so. But the primary import of military support is likely to be the way it conditions the movement's political propaganda.

9. The Vietnam Combination

The Vietnamese situation in its development represented a combination of *two* types of situation: a civil war, and an imperialist intervention.

As we saw, there was something of such a combination before; in the Spanish Civil War, we said, there was also an element of imperialist intervention; but the attitude of revolutionary socialists on the Spanish Civil War was decisively determined by the civil war character, not the other element, which remained subordinate. In the Algerian struggle against French imperialism, there was also a civil war element, but neither side of this civil war (FLN and MNA) was in power or tied up with the imperialist intervention.

The combination of these two elements in Vietnam has been *sui generis* and requires unique analysis.

10. The Civil War Element

If we go back to the point following the expulsion of the French, we find a situation which is plain enough (from the viewpoint of our present problem): an indigenous government in South Vietnam, under Bao Dai and then Ngo Dinh Diem, which, while manipulated into power by and supported by American imperialism has a base of support in all the socially reactionary sectors of the society and is faced with a mass revolutionary threat from within and below.

In 1956 the revolutionary threat materializes with an upsurge of Revolutionary Committees which brings South Vietnam to the brink of a social overturn. At this point, there is no doubt that socialists stand for the political victory of this revolutionary movement (critical political support), though its victory would immediately divide it into a right and left wing. But Diem succeeds in beating back this upsurge, and then of carrying out a reign of intimidation and terror which drives many of the revolutionary elements in the direction of the Communists, and provides part of the context for the rise of the NLF under Communist leadership but with the support of non-Communists.

At this stage, the situation is decisively that of an internal social struggle, going over to civil war as the NLF-Communist leadership mobilizes enemies of the Diem dictatorship to form its fighting cadres. In a third corner are still amorphously organized enemies of the Diem regime who resist being pushed into the arms of the Communists, of which we know best the militant Buddhist wing.

As the armed struggle starts between the Saigon government on the one hand and the NLF-Communist leadership on the other, what we have is a *civil war*. It is a civil war between two reactionary political forces.

On the one hand is the government of the landlord-usurer-compradore-militarist clique of authoritarians, which accepts the role of client of American imperialism but insists on its autonomous rights to carry on its own retrogressive and oppressive social policies even though these embarrass U.S. public relations.

On the other hand is an opposition which is decisively led and controlled by the Communist party — a fact which is not changed politically no matter how many well-intentioned non-Communists are pushed into its ranks by revulsion against Saigon, and no matter how many figure head positions are given to non-Communist fronts.

We know the real political and social program of this Communist leadership as identical with the one already established in North Vietnam, or for that matter in China, allowing for differences in stages in the consolidation of bureaucratic collectivism. We know that this is the same leadership, essentially, as that which made sure murder revolutionary opponents in the past (e.g. organized systematic assassination of Trotskyists) before even fighting the French or collaborators. We know that in *their* order of priorities, they are sooner amenable to making a deal with imperialists than to pursuing collaboration with revolutionary socialists; that for them accommodation with imperialism is a lesser evil than accommodation with a revolutionary democratic movement.

We know, in short, that here we have a leadership bidding for control of the nation which represents a new exploiting social system based on totalitarian collectivism; which bids for power not on behalf of a national reformism but on behalf of *its own social revolution*, which will replace the landlord-usurer-compradore exploitation of the people with their exploitation by a new class of bureaucratic rulers.   In a civil war between aspirants of these old and new exploiting classes, revolutionaries can give no kind of support to either but look to organize independent forces with the possibility of critical support to revolutionary democratic elements like the left wing religio-political currents peculiar to Vietnam.

11. Military Collaboration

In other three-cornered situations that have existed, there has always been the possibility of a relationship, so far unmentioned, which involves neither political nor military support, i.e. *military collaboration*, on a purely practical or tactical basis, with any military force which, at a given moment, is fighting against your enemy.

We refer to such military collaboration as was established by the government of the Russian Revolution in 1918 with Allied elements as against the German forces invading Russia; or, say, military collaboration by independent French partisans with Gaullist forces against the German occupation in World War II; or even the species of military collaboration contemplated by Irish revolutionists with German suppliers of material aid in 1916; all of these being cases involving neither political support nor military support to the side with which such temporary ad hoc collaboration is established.

We can therefore stipulate that, in the complications of the Vietnam situation, such military collaboration would no doubt be a distinct possibility in various contingencies; but, since this ought to go without saying for any such juncture, there will be no need to mention it again.

So much for the element of civil war in Vietnam. While the American intervention remained on the plane of money, material and a relatively small number of military "advisors," the aspect of civil war was clearly and indisputably dominant in the situation — as it was in Spain even though Germany and Italy had more troops in the field there than the U.S. had in Vietnam up to about 1965.

But the *size* of the U.S. intervention at any stage has nothing to do with our *attitude* toward this intervention. With respect to the Vietnam war, we as American socialists are in situation B. From the side of the U.S., what are the politics of which its military intervention are the continuation? Our answer is: This war, on its part, is a continuation of the U.S.'s need to police the world on behalf of the maintenance of world capitalism and its imperialism, as against both popular revolution and the rival power of the Communist camp in the world. From the side of the U.S., it is therefore an unalloyed imperialist intervention.

We are intransigent opponents of this intervention, and of the total U.S. policy in Vietnam, unconditionally. Therefore, we have consistently put in the forefront our demand for the immediate and unconditional withdrawal of the U.S. forces.

12. The Transformation of the Situation

But while the size of the U.S. intervention has nothing to do with our attitude toward this intervention, it is obviously the key to a quite different question, which must be raised in view of the escalation of the U.S. intervention to the present point. It is the same question of fundamental analysis which we raised about the Spanish Civil War; the relative weight of the civil war aspect and the imperialist aspect of a combined situation.

The imperialist element we are talking about here is the direct *American* military intervention. To be sure, Russian and Chinese hands are meddling in the situation too, but we have now had more than one occasion to keep such factors in their proper place. It would be grotesque to put the Russian and Chinese involvement, limited mainly to supplying war materials, on the same plane as a large scale military invasion to impose an alien armed might. To do this would be to do exactly the same thing that the Communist apologists did when Russian tanks imposed their power on Budapest and the journalistic hacks of the pro-Communist press equated this with CIA meddling or Mindszenty's influence in the background. In this case too we have to reject very firmly the kind of sterile political reasoning which subordinates every situation to the pervasive cold war antagonism which exists in the background.

Well then, what is now the relative weight of the civil war aspect and the imperialist element in Vietnam? We do not have any doubt that in (say) 1956 the civil war element was dominant. But in 1968 everyone knows that the U.S. has taken over the brunt of the fighting; no one really pretends that the American military involvement is simply an auxiliary aid to the patriotic army of South Vietnam defending its homeland against invaders; it is commonplace that it is "America's war" now.

Translated into our language, what this says is that the aspect of imperialist intervention has been taking over from the civil war aspect, and it raises the question of *at what point one is duty bound to decide that what began as a predominantly civil war is now predominantly a situation of imperialist invasion.*

Two points about the kind of problem this is:

(1) A decision on this never has been and is not now our greatest priority in point of policy, since we have, right along and never more than now, rightly concentrated our practical work and attention on fighting U.S. intervention in the war; and nothing that we can decide on this point could possibly increase our antiwar activity or intensify our antiwar politics. What it would affect is only certain aspects of what we say propagandistically in the course of this antiwar activity and how we explain it. This makes it worthwhile to clarify the question without inflating its importance.

(2) It is no part of our problem to make a definite determination of exactly at what hour of the day one type of situation changed into another. Since the escalation was a continuum, that is both hopeless and pointless (like the classic problem of at just what instant you become "bald" if you pull your hairs out one by one, or the moment when Russia ceased to be a workers' state.)

The meaningful problem to pose is simply this: at a given point — namely, right now — is it possible to ascertain that the nodal point of change has *already been passed*, and to demonstrate politically that the civil war aspect of the situation has been overshadowed or transcended?

13. The Qualitative Change

If it is possible to do this, it is not only because the quantitative increase in Washington's military operations has clearly brought about the qualitative change in the war which leads one to speak of it as "America's war." The same picture is indicated by a social test, as distinct from simply a military criterion — a social phenomenon which has been growing in the last couple of years and which was *definitively* manifested by the Tet offensive.

This is the fact that the NLF has succeeded in winning such overwhelming allegiance, active or passive, from the South Vietnam population — *not merely "mass support" or even majority support* — as to make it difficult or impossible to consider the Saigon government even as the government of a minority section of the nation in a civil war situation. The offensive revealed it as a government clique separated from any section of the people and existing only because of the U.S.

When an "enemy" can move thousands of troops into a capital city, and organize ammunition depots and military posts, for weeks before an attack, with a whole sector of the population necessarily aware that something is going on, and without a single man, woman or child betraying the massive operation to the official government , then it is not possible to believe that a situation of "civil war" describes the state of affairs. This is a phenomenon that can occur only in the midst of a population that sees the issue as between its "own" people and an alien — as it would have done in Vichy France.

The Tet offensive *revealed* this; it did not bring it about; obviously a preceding stage had been marked by the phony election, for example; but in any case we are interested at this point only in ascertaining that a nodal point *is being passed.*

We have no need to change our political approach in any way: we need only apply it anew to what we perceive as a *new stage* of the Vietnam situation, the stage in which the element of American imperialist intervention has decisively overborne the civil war and now determines the nature of the war. In effect, the NLF already seems to have won political power among the South Vietnamese people. It has long been true that it enjoyed at least dual power in much of the territory; but now it appears that the other power, that of the Saigon military clique, can most accurately be viewed in the same light as the French Vichy regime in association with the German occupation. We had hoped that a revolutionary third force would arise in Vietnam before this happened; we must record that this hope seems to have been disappointed.

As the Vietnam situation moves to such a new stage, the situation tends to resemble the Cuban invasion type of situation more and more.

We are leaving some rubber in our formulation only for one reason: we do not claim to *know* all the facts behind the rush of events in Vietnam, particularly whether or not there are revolutionary elements left in opposition to the Saigon regime that have not gone over in despair to some degree of collaboration with the NLF; in other words, whether an upsurge of independent revolutionary elements is foreclosed or not. We do not propose any resolution about *facts*, especially facts we cannot know. We are not discussing past history but rather rapidly changing realities. All we can try to do is note the *direction* that the situation is moving in, and apply our political analysis to it. There is no need for us to try to do more.

If the case of the NLF is in fact being assimilated with that of the Castro regime under invasion by the U.S., *then it follows that the question of military support is automatically raised,* in exactly the same way we discussed in connection with Cuba.

If we decide this is definitely established, there is little that is concrete that is affected in our politics. Above all, there is not the slightest effect on our position of revolutionary political opposition to all such regimes, whatever their successes.

The victory of the NLF is a hard fact, but no one's victory changes our political opinion of him. We remain revolutionary opponents of the NLF as of the Castro regime, and do not foster illusions about either. We combat glorification of the NLF, such as is met among some left opponents of U.S.

Vietnam policy who think that opposition to American imperialism entails uncritical gilding of its victims, and who wrong headedly use the NLF (for example)
as a symbol of the struggle for Vietnamese self-determination. Such political
glorification of the NLF springs from two quite different sources: (a) Consciously
pro-Communist elements who boost the NLF *because* it is the road to Communist
power. (b) Naive, basically liberal elements who identify the NLF politically with
anti-imperialism through the same uninformed ingenuousness as once promoted
the line that Mao was only an agrarian reformer. They exaggerate the non-
Communist side of the NLF as an argument against U.S. policy, thereby in fact
conceding part of the principle to U.S. anti-Communism.

Telling the truth about the NLF now is also political preparation for the
possible next stage, when the struggle against the bureaucratic collectivist regime
goes to the head of the agenda.

The success of the NLF in Vietnam is due not to the attractive power of
Communism for the Vietnamese people but in spite of it; it is the gift of American
imperialism, which once again showed that it works hand in glove with its Communist rival to convince a people that indigenous Communist domination is the
lesser evil to alien domination as soon as the choice is narrowed down to these
two. The Diems and Kys worked hard, with the help of their American patrons,
to eliminate revolutionary opposition and democratic alternatives. It is the Communists who reaped the fruits of this reactionary policy.

But we have said before, in anticipation of such an eventuality, that even the
definitive victory of the NLF in Vietnam would not be the End-of-the-World for
the Vietnamese people, but only the beginning of a new chapter in the struggle for
social freedom. There are at least three challenges visible from this point to the
consolidation of the Communist power, if we assume the definitive elimination of
the Americans and their clients.

(1) *The Consolidation Crisis.* Whether a postwar government takes the form of
a "coalition government" or a straight NLF government (the difference between
these alternatives is not sharp), the first crisis would come in a showdown between
the Communist leadership and the nationalist elements who had been pushed into
their arms by the imperialists.

We have no special knowledge of the forces involve and therefore cannot be
confident of the result. Only, in the light of past experience, everything we do
know points to the ability of the Communists vis a vis such elements to carry
through the same kind of "salami tactics" against coalition partners as was applied
in Eastern Europe, with the probable eventual consolidation of a monolithic Com-

munist regime as soon as the partners have been digested and eliminated. Still, this leaves out the possibility, even in this stage, of a significant popular resistance to totalitarianism.

(2) *National Communism.* In any case, the Communist forces themselves would immediately face the problems of national relations with North Vietnam (in view of NLF pledges), China and Russia. In view of the indications that the Ho regime itself would, once relieved of military pressure, turn fully toward a national-Communist regime at least as independent as Rumania or North Korea or perhaps Yugoslavia, it is likely that a crisis with a more pro-Moscow or pro-Peking forces would not be racking. There is more of a question mark over relations between an NLF government in the South and the Ho regime in the North, with accompanying greater possibility of a crisis over such differences.

(3) *The Next Revolution.* Most important is the certain development of revolutionary opposition to Communist totalitarianism itself, if not in the immediate postwar stage, when the victors are flushed with success and national prestige, then in the stage after that. A people who have shown such extraordinary tenacity in revolutionary resistance over decades to Western imperialism will not be behind the Polish people in incubating the forces of rebellion against the new masters as against the old.

This revolutionary development can be short circuited mainly by one thing: continued imperialist pressure from the U.S., such as will keep the people still looking to the Communists as their shield against the old world oppressors. So it was that one of Castro's strongest bucklers against discontent at home is the degree of fear still aroused by U.S. threats; and that fear of a West German resurgence of reaction was skillfully used by the Gomulka regime in Poland to quash the dynamism of the Polish revolution of 1956. Communist power still feeds on the crimes of Western imperialism within its empire, just as U.S. reaction feeds on the crimes of the Communist world to keep its discontented bemused with its reactionary anti-Communism.

Therefore a *sine qua non* for any revolutionary development in the world is the curbing of American imperialism and its partners and allies; and the best inspiration that could be given to the peoples oppressed by the bureaucratic collectivist system is the revolutionary struggle and example of the masses on *our* side of the struggle for the world. Our immediate enemy is at home as before.

Berkeley 1969

About the Authors

The late Hal Draper was the author of many books, including the five-volume study of *Karl Marx's Theory of Revolution*, as well as *Socialism from Below* and *Berkeley: The New Student Revolt*. He was also a prominent socialist journalist and editor of the journal *Labor Action* from 1948–1958.

Samuel Farber was born and raised in Marianao, Cuba, and came to the United States in February 1958. He obtained a PhD in sociology from the University of California at Berkeley in 1969 and taught at a number of colleges and universities including UCLA and, most recently, Brooklyn College, where he is a Professor Emeritus of Political Science. His scholarship on Cuba is extensive and includes many articles and several books. Farber was active in the Cuban high school student movement against Fulgencio Batista in the 1950s, and has been involved in socialist politics for more than fifty years.

CPSIA information can be obtained
at www.ICGtesting.com
Printed in the USA
JSHW062324291122
34080JS00004B/6